MW01534774

"In the race of life, some fall a
seek pity for their condition. '
by their God and keep movin§
into our spiritual lives and re1
but that we take Him up on
language of this book, 'Don't just stay down and fallen. Get up and keep moving!' This
book is a must read for everyone who feels the sting of past and present failures and longs
for a way out of the pain."

—*Dr. Joyce R. Aryee,* Founder & Executive Director, Salt and Light Ministries

"Let me give you just two reasons why you should read *Six More Chances.* First, only
someone who has failed—and failed big-time—is really qualified to write a book that takes
a topic such as Failure and somehow magically transforms the mundane into something
truly sublime. Second, every single person on this terrestrial globe can relate to what it
means to fail at something, sometime or other. That is humankind's lot. But it is a rare
individual indeed that can extract beauty out of the bitter ashes of abject failure and
defeat. Dr. Pipim, in relating his own bitter experience with failure, is uniquely qualified
to address the topic. He's been on the mountaintop, in the abyss of the deepest despair,
and is on his way back up toward Zion's hill. Join him, not only as you see yourself
somewhere in this remarkable book, but also as *you* rise to the top. Someone is waiting
for us up there with open arms!"

—*Jerry Stevens, Former Editor,* Christian Record Services

"In an environment where there are so many people whose lives are helpless and hopeless
in dealing with failures and rejection, Dr. Pipim presents a reminder that is so readily
forgotten in today's task-driven culture. In *Six More Chances,* he unveils his soul into
the reader's heart and provides joy in the midst of sorrow, hope in the times of despair
and peace to the brokenhearted. Simple yet complex, conceptual and practical, *Six More
Chances* encourages introspection and incremental development to becoming the person
God would have you be. It's written by an author who speaks from the Word of God to
shift the paradigm from failure to success. This excellent and thought-provoking work
offers an innovative approach that speaks for itself. A must-read for those who have felt
despondency after failure, this book explains that there is another chance, in fact more
than 'Six More Chances.' The author learns of God's restorative process of healing and hope,
which he very eloquently shares with the reader. In sum, *Six More Chances* dispenses
potent medicine for those who have experienced failure and are in need of healing and
restoration."

—*Dr. Edna Andrews Rose,* Clinical Nurse Consultant, Department of Neurology,
The University of Michigan

"*Six More Chances* is a life-changing book. It takes courage and resolute faith to write a book that takes fear out of failure—even the failure of hope, health, and life itself! This insightful yet easy-to-read work will greatly benefit both the religious and non-religious."

—**Dr. Bisi Obadofin,** *Associate Professor, Counseling Psychology, Lagos State University.*

"This is a great book! God has blessed the author's ability to communicate with others through written words. Dr. Pipim has taken a subject we all face often in our lives and has offered encouragement to get up and start over again. That is the gospel in terms many will be able to identify with! The greatest lesson is to keep our eyes on Jesus! Thank you for the book. I will be getting many copies to share with members here."

—**Dan Hall,** *Pastor, Georgia-Cumberland Conference, Georgia*

"Habakkuk 3:19 comes to mind when I reflect on my reading of Dr. Pipim's latest project *Six More Chances: Success in the Midst of Failure.*

The Lord God is my strength, my personal bravery, and my invincible army; He makes my feet like hinds' feet and will make me to walk [not to stand still in terror, but to walk] and make [spiritual] progress upon my high places [of trouble, suffering, or responsibility] (THE AMPLIFIED BIBLE).

"A wondrous work is done when a brother and sister in Christ witness to His grace and mercy in their marriage, express and demonstrate obedience to His call to spread the Good News, and act on the commission to bring comfort to others who are in their own spiritual journeys.

"It is my pleasure to recommend this work, which has been inspired as God has worked His tremendous healing in the lives of Dr. and Mrs. Pipim. May all who read it find release from bondage of yesterday's sin, through God's mighty work of healing. May those who suffer find the hope that only God can give, through others who have walked the stony path to the foot of the cross, where they, in humble supplication, have received forgiveness for their sins. May all who seek Him, in faith and obedience, find that they are washed by the blood of the Lamb, Who died to save us all from our sins."

—**Julia Chappelle-Thomas,** *Editorial Consultant, Missouri*

"Only a man who has been delivered from the bottom can rightly tell how it is down there, and how to get out. But we do not want to talk about our failures because it quarantines us from what we all crave so much—the adulation and applause of the world. Many therefore lack the will to move on because they have failed and cannot talk about it. The author has, through his latest book, used the painful privilege of having been down there to lead souls who have failed back to God.

"Dr. Pipim offers *Six More Chances*, a product of his bitter experience, as a stepping-stone out of the dark, for all who share a similar experience. It is a must-read for everyone struggling with failure. And quite frankly, that's all of us."

—**Paul Ogaga,** *Realtor; CEO, Estarpal NIG Ltd., & President, ALIVE Nigeria*

M6RE CHANCES

SAMUEL **KORANTENG-PIPIM**, PhD

M6RE CHANCES

SIX

~ SUCCESS ~
IN THE MIDST OF
FAILURE

E**A**GLES
ONLINE
BOOKS

ANN ARBOR, MICHIGAN

DEDICATION

~

Giselle Mahoro,
Your graduation assignment laid
the foundation for this book.

2011 GYC Attendees,
Your dedication and prayers inspired
the production of this work.

&

**Young People & Readers
Around the World**
That you may learn lessons from my failure and be
encouraged by my faith and resilience.

EAGLES
O N L I N E
B O O K S

Six More Chances
Copyright © 2012 by Samuel Koranteng-Pipim, Ph.D.
Published by EAGLESonline Books, Ann Arbor, Michigan, U.S.A.
All Rights Reserved
First Printing, February 2012

Layout and Cover Design: Simon Eitzenberger, *www.desim.de*
Cover Photo: Istockphoto/Clint Spencer's Photography, (www.clintspencer.com)
Copy Editors: Jerry Stevens & Julia Chappelle-Thomas

Hardcover: ISBN 978-1-890014-14-8
Softcover: ISBN 978-1-890014-15-5
E-Book: ISBN 978-1-890014-16-2

For your personal copy of *Six More Chances*, or for additional copies,
contact your local Christian book store or contact:
Remnant Publications, 649 East Chicago Road, Coldwater, MI 49036, U.S.A.
Tel. 1-800-423-1319
www.remnantpublications.com

For quantity discounts to churches, schools, or groups, contact the author through the above
information, or for more information, visit:
info@EAGLESonline.org; or *www.TheWoundedEagleBooks.com*

Koranteng-Pipim, Samuel
Six More Chances: Success In the Midst of Failure / Samuel Koranteng-Pipim
1. Success and Failure—Christianity
2. Spiritual Growth
3. Religion & Spirituality—Christian Life
4. Motivational & Inspirational
I. Title

Printed in the United States of America

"A RIGHTEOUS MAN
MAY FALL SEVEN TIMES
AND RISE AGAIN..."

— Proverbs 24:16, NKJV

CONTENTS

~

INTRODUCTION

~

Everyone wants to be a success. No one purposely sets out to be a failure. This may explain why bookstores are full of popular "How to Succeed Manuals" on every conceivable subject.

While failure is not necessarily the most popular subject, it is one to which we all need to pay attention. Why? Because failure is one of the few things all of us excel at. And yet, this subject of our "expertise" is seldom addressed.

Could it be that the secret to success lies in learning important lessons from failure?

SUCCESS AND FAILURE

We have a lot to learn from both success and failure. *Success* achieves what was planned or attempted. As a result, it is often rewarded with applause, approval, riches, position, and other expressions of recognition. Generally speaking, people tend to measure *Success* by a yardstick they variously label Prestige, Favor, Status, Wealth, or Power, etc.

On the other hand, *Failure*, which may be viewed as the opposite of *Success*, deviates from expected and desired results. Other names for *Failure* include: Defeat, Loss, Mistakes, Faults, Missteps, Setbacks, Scandals, etc. Unlike *Success*, *Failure* is generally frowned upon.

Success is the celebrity who attracts much attention. *Failure* is the outcast, the one often blamed, rejected, scorned and punished by society—whether secular or religious.

We each want to be a *Success*, but *Failure* tends to stand in the way. In fact, in our own lives there are more records of our failures than our successes. And yet, when we get to talk about ourselves, it is much easier to talk about our successes than sharing our failures.

Because we seldom talk about our failures, many people out there think they are alone in their struggles with failure. They're crying out for help, but they cannot seem to reach out to us. They think we're so perfect—so successful—or so spiritual that we will not understand, but rather condemn, them. So they choose to hide their painful struggles with failure along with the rest of us, pretending all is well.

> FAILURE IS ONE OF THE FEW THINGS
> ALL OF US EXCEL AT. AND YET,
> THIS SUBJECT OF OUR "EXPERTISE"
> IS SELDOM ADDRESSED.

I became fully aware of this desperate need after I experienced a major failure in my life. (In the course of this book, I'll share a little more on this.) After that experience of failure and my public ownership of the same, many people started confiding in me about their own battles and about other issues.

I discovered that there is a very large—but secret—world of failures out there—in society, as well as in the church. These individuals long to be free from their burden of failure. They seek to know how to relate responsibly to their failures. They want to experience victory over their failures. They want to know the secret of *Success*.

I have decided to write about failure in the hope that *Six More Chances* will offer some clarity into a commonly overlooked subject, offer hope to those who have failed, and lead them from *Failure* to *Success*.

In this Introduction I briefly describe the secret world of *Failure*, revealing the two faces of *Failure*. Then I point to the upside of *Failure*, mentioning some valuable contributions of *Failure*. Finally, I briefly summarize what this book is all about.

LET'S TALK ABOUT FAILURE

I mentioned earlier that, whereas *Success* is a celebrity, *Failure* is an outcast. Well, that is not the full story. For *Failure* has two faces, depending on whether the exploiter is another or himself.

The Failures of Others

Failure lives in the closet most of the time. The only time he receives a lot of attention is when he emerges from the closets of *others*. When that happens, Failure becomes instantly famous. He is feverishly sought after to appear as a welcome guest on news headlines. He vies for attention as the talk of the town or at many dinner tables, and he boosts the ratings of blogs and Web sites that seek pride of place in the cyberworld.

Failure—that is, the failures of others—also becomes the object of scholarly research, and in religious circles he is often known as a Cain, an Achan, a Jezebel, a Judas, or even as an Ananias or Sapphira, who committed the unpardonable sin against the Holy Spirit, and hence were doomed to eternal damnation.

Failure also receives a lot of attention from other individuals or interest groups. On one hand, critics are interested in Failure because it enables them to justify their personal or ideological opposition to Failure. On the other hand, the jealous or envious show great interest in Failure because this permits them to exploit his plight in order to shift the spotlight momentarily to their own successes—recognition of which they think they have been unfairly denied.

There are also those who show obsessive interest in Failure (that of others, of course), even though they lack adequate knowledge of the facts surrounding Failure. In this category are the pious and the all-knowing professionals and/or experts in the psychology of human behavior. Many of these specialists genuinely want to help Failure and those affected by his actions, but their zeal without knowledge often results in hurting many.

Though I describe Failure with the generic "he," Failure is actually gender-neutral, race-neutral, and age-neutral.

As far as occupation is concerned, Failure—that is, "failure of others," the generic he—defies socioeconomic class segregation. But his fame increases when he identifies with high-profile professionals (politicians, ministers, sports and movie personalities, etc.). Not infrequently, we are privileged to have Failure as one of our family members, well connected with important personalities. His siblings include:

- FINANCIAL FAILURES
- MARRIAGE / RELATIONSHIP FAILURES
- ACADEMIC FAILURES
- BUSINESS FAILURES
- PROFESSIONAL FAILURES
- HEALTH FAILURES
- SPIRITUAL FAILURES
- ET CETERA

Failure can be very insecure or cruel, depending on how you look at him. He can be a coward or a monster. If not quickly arrested, he often becomes a walking time bomb, ticking away to his own destruction and that of others around. He rarely gives up a fight no matter how wounded, until he has brought his victims down to nothingness.

Our Own Failures

But when it comes to our own failures, Failure becomes a different person. She's not as bad as "the failures of others." She makes no mistakes at all because she is a perfect and a very spiritual person.

I refer to this particular Failure as a "she," not just to be fair in an equal-opportunity world, but also because she is a very tenderhearted person, one who gets hurt very easily. She is the other face of Failure.

Given the human tendency to negatively judge people who have failed, we often don't want to talk about her—that is, about our own failures. We are expert journalists, researchers, counselors, and judges on other people's failures, but hardly experts on our own. Indeed, we are so secretive and defensive about her that we may be unable to recognize her, or even consider her a precious asset. In some cases we may even parade her in public, but never as Failure; for we identify her as Success.

The stigma that is often attached to Failure leads us to guard sacredly the circumstances of our failures. Even though "the failures of others" are fair game, *our own failures* are secrets never to be made public or spoken aloud. Hence we've developed an elaborate culture of hiding mistakes, which is at the foundation of many of the myths about victims and abuses. She—our aggregate failure—is a victim. She has been abused and therefore deserves attention.

The truth though, is that like her, we all have become specialists in hypocrisy. From two Greek words, *hypo* (under) and *krinei'* (to decide or distinguish), the word "hypocrisy" literally means to make a decision to hide something under a false appearance. That's how we often deal with our failures and mistakes.

And we've honed the tools for our expertise in hypocrisy: We conceal *our* failures and mistakes by cover-ups, excuses, denials, and accusations often displayed in our outrage or righteous indignation against other people's failures. In today's "culture of victims," we've all become specialists in blaming others, circumstances, Satan, and even God.

Hypocrisy is nothing less than a lie, discouraging us from owning up to our failures and asking for help and encouragement when we need it most. We fear what people will think of us if they know how sinful our failures really are.

> WE ARE EXPERT JOURNALISTS, RESEARCHERS, COUNSELORS, AND JUDGES ON OTHER PEOPLE'S FAILURES, BUT HARDLY EXPERTS ON OUR OWN.

But we ought not treat Failure as an embarrassment that needs to be hidden underneath. Failure is not a minority or an endangered species requiring special protection. We don't need a census or poll to know that there are (and have been) more failures than successes. We are surrounded by abundant physical and archival evidence that attest to this fact.

The two-faced Failure described thus far, is what often comes to mind when we think of Failure—whether ours or others'. Because of the pain, costliness, and shame associated with Failure's actions, virtually everyone fears Failure—whether a personal, professional, or spiritual failure. Failure—whether personified as "other people's failures" or "our own failures"—holds many hostages. And out of despair and hopelessness, this Failure has often driven its discouraged victims to commit suicide.

Another Kind of Failure

But there is another kind of Failure we should really get to know. Not the pain, hurt, and hypocrisy of the previously described Failure, but *praiseworthy* Failure. It is the Failure who knows how to fail well—how to transform its defeats and mistakes into accomplishments. It is the Failure who becomes a Success.

He is a sage. The one who has had to pay heavy tuition to gain the theoretical and experiential knowledge that few have. The one who defies all odds to wiggle out of the closet, escape hands that threaten to snuff life out of it, and get back to a steady trot on the road to success. The one that pays special attention to what many would miss, packs his lessons carefully in a bag securely fastened to his body, and starts the "forward ever, backward never" pilgrimage toward success.

This particular kind of Failure has also been around for a long time and has a wealth of knowledge to impart. It is expedient that we visit this Failure, sit at his feet, and learn some valuable lessons. We have nothing to lose, and a whole lot to gain, by taking him up on the offer to impart freely that which he paid heavily to learn.

LET'S LEARN FROM FAILURE

The wisest man who ever lived, King Solomon, said: "It is better to go to a house of mourning than to go to a house of feasting, because that is the end [destiny] of every man, and the living takes it to heart." (ECCLESIASTES 7:2 [NASB]).

Paraphrasing this passage in terms of failure and success, we might reword this to say:

> "It is better to go to a house of Failure than to go to a house of Success, because Failure is the experience of every man, and he has much to teach the wise, who sit at his feet to learn his valuable lessons."

Another way of stating it is to employ the quote popularized by a 2007 Walt Disney movie, *Meet the Robinsons*: "From failure, you learn. From success, not so much."

The basic idea is that though failure can be painful, *failing well can breed success*. When properly handled, failure can be a friend—an aid—to success. For, not only does failure enable us to know what is undesirable or doesn't work, it also gives us an opportunity to try new approaches and discover solutions that would have been missed but for those failures.

Indeed, some of the greatest men and women who ever lived triumphed over their failures. The best and most successful companies are those that embrace their mistakes and learn from them. Many breakthroughs in research and inventions are sometimes the result of failures.

And even in the case of spiritual failures, some great men and women have been made only after going through major failures (think of Bible characters such as Abraham, Miriam, Aaron, Moses, Elijah, David, Peter, Mary Magdalene, Paul, etc.). Having confessed their failures to God, these individuals learned from their mistakes and were subsequently used, sometimes in even mightier ways.

The Upside of Failure

In the non-spiritual realm, Failure's experience of trying and failing (or, as we say, "trial and error," and even euphemize as "experimentation") is known to be the heartbeat of innovation and the foundation of many vocations.

In an article, aptly titled "The Upside of Failure: The Dividends of Understanding and Embracing Your Failures," Tim Eyre explains why we must embrace failure as a friend. Why *"failure merely represents a bump in the road toward success and should not be regarded as defeat."* He explains:

Chemists, for example, often must conduct experiment after experiment before they uncover the correct formula, and the same is true for many other science-related professions. Likewise, the most celebrated chefs in the world routinely tweak their recipes and test new flavors in their dishes; along the way, lots of food gets burned and/or trashed. In addition, physicians may conduct numerous tests or try various treatments before settling on a diagnosis. But your average chemist does not view the first 20 failed attempts leading up to the 21st successful one in a negative light. Famous chefs don't fret over the failed recipes that precede their masterpieces. And we don't consider doctors failures if it takes time and multiple attempts to get the answer right. Instead, in these professions, failure is accepted as a normal part of the process toward achievement.[1]

Yes, there are failures in human endeavors that result from courageous risk-taking. These undertakings were conceived and executed in a smart way, but the outcome was not what was expected and desired. These kinds of failures are understandable, if not laudable, for they can teach us valuable lessons.

But these realities by no means suggest that all failures deserve praise.

> THROUGH THE ENABLING GRACE OF GOD,
> WE CAN ALL SUCCEED THROUGH FAILURE.

The Downside of Failure

There are many other kinds of failure that deserve no honor, though they too may lead to success, if their disgrace is acknowledged in a manner to forge success from it. Such failures are of many kinds, but generally stem from pride and selfishness that often result in poor judgment or a lack of thoughtful preparation. Such failures often involve risk-taking that is inexcusable. Unfortunately, such failures do exist. In fact, a majority of failures fall into this category. And when they do occur, judgment upon them can understandably be harsh, if not entirely retributive.

But the worst criticism against inexcusable failures goes to those resulting from spiritual failure. Sin. To excuse or explain it is to justify it.

But it should be stressed that even in the case of spiritual failure—inexcusable failure—God can use such failures as lessons for growth and change. When properly handled, those who have failed spiritually can become successful again because of God's amazing grace—His forgiving, transforming, and restorative grace.

God's ability to convert spiritually incurred failures into blessings applies to all categories of sin—whether or not the circumstances leading to it may appear understandable. For example, though still sin, it is quite understandable when a person acts rashly in a moment of extreme provocation (like Moses striking the rock). However, we cannot excuse failure that is premeditated and repetitious (such as Samson's and Peter's).

In the case of Peter, for example, Jesus had warned him that it would happen. So he knew ahead of time to take adequate precautions. Also his denial of his Lord was a deliberate act (it was an intentional lie). Worse yet, Peter's spiritual failure was a repetitious error (three times denying Christ). To put it bluntly, the spiritual failure of Peter was an intentional, willful, repetitious act of sinning. It cannot be put on a par with Moses'.

But here, and this is the part that is important to remember, the God Who eagerly forgave even Peter's failure, is just as eager to forgive the worst type of spiritual failure. Now, if God can somehow use deliberate spiritual failures, such as that experienced by Peter, to change his life and restore him to usefulness again, then He can surely use the other less dramatic kinds of failure that are common to our experience as well.

DEALING WITH FAILURE

Six More Chances does not promote or condone any type of failure. This book, however, acknowledges that failure, whether spiritual or otherwise, does occur; and we must relate to it responsibly so that we can prevail over it.

When failure (in any of its forms) occurs, it need not be dreaded to the point of despair, nor treated as an outcast in a pit of discouragement. Through the enabling grace of God, we can all succeed through failure. This book will explain why and how.

There may be other future works on different aspects of failure. Right now, however, in *Six More Chances*, I have decided to write on the neglected, if not scorned, subject of failure to offer a way forward when we encounter instances of failure.

The ideas for these works were developed when, after my failure, I took time off to "sit in the dark" as it were, to reflect on what happened to me and the lessons I could derive from them. In the form of short "Songs in the Dark" thought nuggets, I have shared some of these ideas with my Facebook friends and on my apologetic Web site.[2]

In this particular work, I'm providing a philosophy of failure that enables us to turn our failures into successes.

⌐ CHAPTER 1—Offers practical guidelines to overcome failure— any kind of failure—and transform it into success. The content of this chapter expands upon a graduation address I gave at a private graduation event at The University of Michigan.

⌐ CHAPTER 2—Briefly discusses the sources for our knowledge of what constitutes true success and failure, gleans some inspirational thoughts from the past, addresses the question as to whether or not we should learn from success or failure, and concludes by pointing to a Model of success.

⌐ CHAPTER 3—Considers the ultimate failure in life—the failure of our dreams, hopes, and life itself—through death. Loss—especially of a loved one—is another word for failure. But should such failure be final? The chapter explains what ultimate failure really is and how to triumph over it.

⌐ CHAPTER 4—Concludes with another failure we all confront: personal or spiritual failure. How do we deal with it? What is the one secret to success when one faces failure at any level? And why should we be hopeful under the failures we face? It is this chapter that provides an explanation of the "Six More Chances" in the title of this book.

⌐ POSTSCRIPT—Provides an insightful last word on the content of this book. Written by a person who is very close to the author, it describes the pains and hopes that birthed this book, and affirms that, despite the tragedy and consequences of the failure that resulted in this book, there is still reason to be thankful. Our hearts can still be full of gratitude.

Because of the overlapping nature of the chapters, it is inevitable that there should be a certain amount of repetition of some ideas. These are designed to augment and supplement salient points being addressed. Notice the disclaimer of the apostle Paul: "It is no trouble for me to write the same things to you again, and it is a safeguard for you" (PHILIPPIANS 3:1).

Six More Chances will argue that instead of wallowing in self-pity on account of failure, we must adopt certain attitudes and mindsets that will move us beyond failure. Even in the case of spiritual failure, we must embrace failure as an opportunity to learn, to reorder our lives, and allow the Lord to help us bounce back.

The ultimate goal of the book is to assure all that none need to be discouraged on account of failure, for God has made more than adequate provision for us in Christ. As you're going to discover, our God is not just a God of "second chances" but also a God of "six more chances." Nay, a God of "much more than six more chances." He provides opportunity for us to keep getting up when we fall. Through Christ, grace is available to all who are battling with their failures. Connected with Him, there can be no failure.

—*Samuel Koranteng-Pipim, PhD*
January 1, 2012

"WE ARE HARD-PRESSED ON EVERY SIDE,
YET NOT CRUSHED; WE ARE PERPLEXED,
BUT NOT IN DESPAIR; PERSECUTED,
BUT NOT FORSAKEN; STRUCK DOWN,
BUT NOT DESTROYED."
—*2 Corinthians 4:8, 9, NKJV*

CHAPTER 1

⌐

SUCCESS
IN THE MIDST OF
FAILURE

Thoughts From an Expert on Failure

(*A Graduation Address*)

I. THANK YOU, GISELLE

It is said that there are three important days in a person's life. Unfortunately, graduation from school is not one of them.

- ⌐ 1. THE DAY YOU ARE **HATCHED**
- ⌐ 2. THE DAY YOU ARE **MATCHED**
- ⌐ 3. THE DAY YOU ARE **DISPATCHED**

The day you are *hatched* is the day you are born; the day you are *matched* is the day you get married, and the day you are *dispatched* is the day you die. Somewhere in between these three important days, we have managed to fit in the day of our graduation—kindergarten graduation, elementary (primary) school graduation, high school graduation, college and university graduation, and who knows what other kinds of graduation.

Consistent with the above rhymes, I'll describe graduation as the day you are BATCHED (the process by which we assemble a group of students in batches—in this case, those who have accomplished a specific number of course requirements—so as to constitute a new sociological group called graduates).

We've all been summoned here by this special occasion of the batching of Giselle. From this day forward she's going to be part of this year's graduating class from The University of Michigan. She's going to be inducted into the elite group of U of M alums, and part of the fraternity of professionals with degrees in molecular biology. We're all delighted to be here to share the joy of this special occasion.[1]

Not too long ago, I received Giselle's e-mail invitation to this event. The invitation reads in part:

> I was wondering if you would be willing to give a 15-min. speech on "Success in the midst of failure"? I know the evening will be about celebrating success but I think it's important to be reminded that failures will come, and knowing how to "get back up" is essential.

I responded immediately:

> What an honor to speak in my new capacity as an expert on failure. ☺ I'd be more than delighted. I'll be out of town from Dec. 15–18th. But I'll be flying in by 2:00 PM, so it should give me enough time to be there. Congratulations in advance.

Giselle may have been a little embarrassed by my reference to myself as "an expert on failure." Perhaps she thought I was offended that she had asked me to speak on failure, since I had experienced failure earlier in the year—a failure that resulted in my resignation as Director of Public Campus Ministries. Thus, Giselle e-mailed back:

> I'm so glad you can make it. *You are not an expert on failure. On the contrary, you are such an expert on success that you somehow manage to succeed even in failure.* ☺ Thank you so much and I hope to see you soon.

Don't worry Giselle, I don't mind at all being an "expert on failure." I prefer that title to being "an expert on success." *For if failure is education,*

then I am one of the most educated persons here. And I am in very good company.
For what you may have forgotten is that WE are all graduates from that same school.

I am an expert on failure because, unlike many others, my education in failure is more costly and is public knowledge. But as you're going to discover, failure is the twin of success. Thus, I'm also one of the most optimistic in your midst, believing that something good will come out of my failure. I'll share with you how you also can succeed through your respective failures of life.

Seriously, though, the reason Giselle invited me to speak on failure is because she knows I'm writing a book, not only on the lessons I've learned from my own personal failure, but also on lessons we can learn from the failures of some well-known Bible characters.

> FOR IF FAILURE IS EDUCATION, THEN I AM
> ONE OF THE MOST EDUCATED PERSONS HERE.
> AND I AM IN VERY GOOD COMPANY.
> FOR WHAT YOU MAY HAVE FORGOTTEN IS
> THAT WE ARE ALL GRADUATES FROM
> THAT SAME SCHOOL.

GENERAL COMMENTS

Since Giselle has requested me to speak on a specific topic, allow me to first make four or five general comments before jumping into my assignment. They are comments I often give at all of my graduation speeches.

1. DON'T BE AN ILLITERATE GRADUATE.

When you graduate today, and stop learning tomorrow, you'll become an illiterate the next day. There are many graduates in the world today, who for all practical intents and purposes are functional illiterates. Don't increase the population of that group.

2. DON'T EQUATE A DEGREE WITH AN EDUCATION.

An academic degree and true education are not necessarily the same. You can have an impressive degree, even from a prestigious institution, and yet not be educated. I am sometimes embarrassed by many people who have degrees, and even call themselves "Doctors" in one area or another, and yet have not even a teaspoon of true knowledge or education.

And may I say that, even in our church, it is becoming a plague among ministers. Everyone is a Doctor. In Africa, this is even more nauseating, as pastors get offended when you don't refer to them as "Pastor-Doctor So-and-So." The truth of the matter is, though they hold the degrees, some of them are empty calories. There are ordinary church members who have no academic degrees and yet are more educated in practical knowledge and in things of God.

My point is, don't be infatuated by the degree that has just now been conferred upon you. A degree is not necessarily the same as education.

3. TRUE EDUCATION IS A FITNESS FOR LIFE—HERE AND ETERNITY.

We need to expand upon our concept of education. I like what E. G. White says in this respect:

"Our ideas of education take too narrow and too low a range. There is need of a broader scope, a higher aim. *True education means more than the pursual of a certain course of study. It means more than a preparation for the life that now is. It has to do with the whole being, and with the whole period of existence possible to man. It is the harmonious development of the physical, the mental, and the spiritual powers. It prepares the student for the joy of service in this world and for the higher joy of wider service in the world to come.* (EDUCATION, P. 13.1)*

---

* NOTE: E. G. White (1827-1915) is considered the most widely translated American author. Her works have been published in approximately 150 languages. Although her formal schooling ended at age 9, she wrote more than 100,000 pages on a wide variety of practical topics. Guided by the Holy Spirit, she exalted Jesus and pointed to Scripture as the basis for her faith. For more on her works, see, pp. 213-214, endnote 4. In this book, references to E. G. White's works are from the standard English editions of her published writings. See, https://egwwritings.org/.

4. CONSIDER DEDICATING PART OF YOUR LIFE TO BECOMING A MISSIONARY.

This university was where the Peace Corps volunteer movement was launched by John F. Kennedy (March 1960). It challenged a generation of young idealistic students to go to different parts of the world and help in great humanitarian causes.

In essence, JFK was calling for men and women who could go abroad and serve as "missionaries."

It is this same kind of challenge I place before young people when I ask them to dedicate a year of their lives and become missionaries. This is why, from the very first year we established CAMPUS, we made the missionary training program a vital part of it.[2]

And over the years, students have come from major universities in the country—including Princeton, Stanford, Harvard, and MIT—and around the world to receive training and go back to impact their campuses and their worlds. They are not only sacrificing one year of their education to volunteer as students on secular universities in Michigan but are also paying significant tuition and boarding fees to attend. And I want you to also consider serving as a missionary.[3]

The truth is, every one of us has been called to be a missionary wherever God has placed us,[4] and in whatever profession we find ourselves—business, law, medicine, teaching, etc. As we're told, "Christ may be represented in all lawful callings."[5]

But my challenge to you is that, for a limited period of time, consider taking some time off from your regular vocation and go to a needed area and volunteer as a missionary. There is no greater and more meaningful internship than serving as a missionary. Give serious consideration to setting a year or two apart to serve as a missionary—anywhere around the world, including CAMPUS.

5. DON'T FORGET TO CONTRIBUTE MILLIONS OF DOLLARS TO CAMPUS.

I don't need to remind you that CAMPUS needs your help. And you know it will employ wisely your resources to advance the cause of God and humanity. CAMPUS has given birth to powerful grassroots movements, such as GYC, ALIVE, STRIDE, and others. So, here's my pitch: One day, when the Lord blesses you with a good job and you get to marry a rich billionaire, don't forget to contribute substantially to CAMPUS.

On this general note, I'd like to congratulate you on this occasion of earning a degree in molecular biology from this great university. I know the glory goes to the Lord, but you allowed yourself to be used by Him. Thank you for enriching our lives while you were studying here. I trust the Lord will be with you in the next phase of your life.

As a gift for your graduation, I have an autographed copy of one of my books for you. It is your first reading assignment. Remember, if you graduate today and stop studying tomorrow, you'll become an illiterate the next day. I don't want you to be an illiterate graduate.

And now, let me say a few words on the topic you've requested me to speak on.

> IF YOU GRADUATE TODAY
> AND STOP STUDYING TOMORROW,
> YOU'LL BECOME AN
> ILLITERATE THE NEXT DAY.

A Stroke of Wisdom

It's a stroke of wisdom (or remarkable) for you to conceive the idea of reflecting on failure, even as we celebrate your success. Only an excellent graduate from The University of Michigan can conceive such an idea! For we cannot celebrate success without reflecting on failure. There's a relationship between the two.

"Success is on the same road as failure; success is just a little further down the road."

—*Jack Hyles*

What this means is that in arriving at this destination today, you passed through some failures along the way. Yet you prevailed over them.

You see, success is meaningless if there is no possibility of failure. Failure and success are relatives. Though different, the two go hand to hand. And each instructs us about the other. This is why, though the Bible talks about overcoming or living victorious lives, much of the entire Book is devoted to recounting the failures of its heroes.

Therefore, Giselle is wise in reminding us that although today is about celebrating her success, "it's important to be reminded that failures will come, and knowing how to 'get back up' is essential." I'll now proceed to say a few words on the topic assigned to me.

Thank you, Giselle, for giving me the honor to speak at your graduation event.

II. SUCCESS IN THE MIDST OF FAILURE

What I'm about to say on failure has to do with failure in all aspects of life—whether academic, professional, family, or spiritual. In order to transform our failures into success, we need to do certain things. I'll mention ten as we move on.

1. Have a Different Perspective on Failure

Success begins with a healthy view of failure. We need to view failure differently. Scriptures tell us that "as a man thinks in his heart, so is he" (PROVERBS 23:7). Thus, the way we view failure can determine whether or not we succeed.

One dictionary defines failure as:

1. A LACK OF SUCCESS IN SOMETHING, OR AN UNSUCCESSFUL ATTEMPT AT DOING SOMETHING
2. SOMETHING THAT FALLS SHORT OF WHAT IS REQUIRED OR EXPECTED
3. SOMEBODY WHO OR SOMETHING THAT IS UNSUCCESSFUL

Accordingly, when we think of failure, we typically have in mind defeat, a huge blunder, a loss, etc. There seems to be a certain finality to these definitions. But in order to succeed through failure, we need to have a completely different perspective or understanding of failure. Our thinking or definition must change.

Think carefully about the following perspectives on failure:

"Failure is an event, never a person; an attitude, not an outcome."
—*William D. Brown*

The fact that you have failed an exam or job interview (an event) doesn't mean you're a failure (failure is not a person). Failure is not an outcome (e.g., not passing a class, a loss of business, a breakup of a relationship, loss of health, etc.); it is an attitude (how you deal with it). The bottom line is, never think you're a failure. You may have failed in something, but it does not mean you're a failure.

"There is no failure. Only feedback."
—*Robert Allen*

See failure as a feedback—an input on your performance thus far. The feedback tells you how to proceed in the future. You can also view failure in other positive ways:

"Look at failure as a stumble that prevents a fall."
—*SKP*

"Failure is the cloud that temporarily hides the sun.
It is not the death or obliteration of the sun."
—*SKP*

"Failure is a detour, not a dead-end street."
—*Zig Ziglar*

"Failure is the pot containing the seeds of success."
—*SKP*

"Failure is only the opportunity to begin again more intelligently."
—*Henry Ford*

"Failure only means you haven't succeeded yet."
—*Henry Ford*

"Failure is the condiment that gives success its flavor."
—*Truman Capote*

"Failure is not the falling down, but the staying down."
—*Mary Pickford*

What is common in all the above views or perspectives on failure is that failure is not—or ought not be—permanent. You can always bounce back: back to success. Failure can be the road to success.

This mindset, this perspective, is critical if you are to succeed through failure. But there's more.

2. Recognize That You're Not Alone in Failure

As far as life is concerned, failure is the rule rather than the exception. Even though we may not like it, the tragic fact is that failure is the common lot of fallen humanity. Ever since the Fall of Adam and Eve, human beings have always failed in the world. And until Jesus comes again to make all things new, there will be failures—small and big failures, secret and public failures, and those with minor and major consequences.

Regardless of the nature of the failures, one inescapable fact will always remain: Failure will always be with us, and though you may not want to accept or admit it, you are going to fail—even if you have thus far escaped failure.

If you do fail, be encouraged by the fact that you are not the only person who ever failed. Others before you have failed, there are many in your day who have failed, and long after you're gone there will be many more who fail. There is nothing unique about your failure. What ought to be important, as far as failure is concerned, is what you do about your failure.

"In a world flagrant with the failures of civilization, what is there particularly immortal about our own?"
—*G. K. Chesterton*

In fact, the Bible offers us an impressive list of characters who once failed. Even though we're accustomed to referring to them as "Saints" (St. Peter, St. John, St. Paul, etc.), a study of their lives will reveal instances where they failed very miserably. Even those whose failures are not recorded in Scripture (e.g., Elisha, Daniel, etc.) all failed. For the Bible tells us that "all have sinned..." *All* includes everyone, except Christ.

With the exception of our Lord Jesus Christ, every single Bible character sustained some major spiritual failures in the course of life. In fact, we would never have even known about some of God's well-known eagles—the heroes and heroines of the Bible—if it hadn't been for the fact that they failed—sometimes multiple times—and ultimately gained victory to the point of spiritual excellence.

The focus of Scripture on the failures of its notable Bible characters should be both a warning and a source of encouragement to us who live today: We can be educated by their failures:

> The pen of inspiration, true to its task, tells us of the sins that overcame Noah, Lot, Moses, Abraham, David, and Solomon, and that even Elijah's strong spirit sank under temptation during his fearful trial. Jonah's disobedience and Israel's idolatry are faithfully recorded. Peter's denial of Christ, the sharp contention of Paul and Barnabas, the failings and infirmities of the prophets and apostles, are all laid bare by the Holy Ghost, Who lifts the veil from the human heart. There before us lie the lives of the believers, with all their faults and follies, which are intended as a lesson to all the generations following them. If they had been without foible they would have been more than human, and our sinful natures would despair of ever reaching such a point of excellence. But seeing where they struggled and fell, where they took heart again and conquered through the grace of God, we are encouraged, and led to press over the obstacles that degenerate nature places in our way.[6]

To succeed through failure you need to recognize that you don't own the patent right to failure. You're not the first to fail, and neither will you be the last. Take comfort in the fact that in your failures, you share company with the greatest men and women who ever lived, who failed in life, and who, by the grace of God, managed to succeed through their failures.

> TO SUCCEED THROUGH FAILURE YOU NEED
> TO RECOGNIZE THAT YOU DON'T OWN
> THE PATENT RIGHT TO FAILURE.

3. Believe That Your Failure Can Lead to Your Success

Don't be frightened by failure. It can lead to your success. Some of the greatest accomplishments were achieved by individuals who failed, some many times over and some very seriously. Let me illustrate with three individuals, one each from the 18th, 19th, and 20th centuries:

(A) 18TH CENTURY: BENJAMIN FRANKLIN (1706–1790) was among the most talented and multifaceted personalities of this world—past and present included. He is known for many famous quotes and proverbs, some of which may have been born from his observations on failures in life. For example,

"Early to bed, early to rise, makes a man healthy, wealthy, and wise"

"An apple a day keeps the doctor away."

"Three may keep a secret if two of them are dead."

Benjamin Franklin contributed hugely to the world by giving to it his many useful inventions at no cost, refusing to own patents on any invention.[7] Of his many inventions, he's well known for his work in electricity. What many do not know, however, is that his contribution to our knowledge of electricity was the result of his learning from his mistakes or failures.

In his first five years of conducting electricity experiments, Ben Franklin did not make much use of higher mathematics, since he was notably deficient in the subject. Rather, all his early experiments were done by hand, by trial and error: learning from one failure after another.

Also, he was nearly killed by his early experiments with lightning; he survived only because he luckily didn't receive a strong enough charge.

Twice he was knocked senseless: once when he attempted to treat a paralyzed man with electric shock, and another time preparing to kill a turkey by electric shock.

Although he's well known for being one of the greatest inventors who lived, this is what Benjamin Franklin said about failure.

"I didn't fail the test, I just found 100 ways to do it wrong."
—*Benjamin Franklin*

(B) 19TH CENTURY: THOMAS A. EDISON (1847–1931) was an American inventor and businessman. He is one of most prolific inventors in history. He invented the microphone, the phonograph, the incandescent light, the storage battery, talking movies, and more than 1,000 other things. During his lifetime, Edison was awarded 1,368 separate and distinct patents. He died at age 84 on October 18th, 1931—on the anniversary date of his invention of the incandescent bulb.

During his lifetime, Edison experienced many failures in his experiments, but never thought of giving up until he succeeded. Here's what he also said about failure, and its relationship with success.

"I have not failed. I've just found 10,000 ways that won't work."
—*Thomas A. Edison*
[The idea is that even if you try and fail, it doesn't mean that you didn't learn something.]

"Many of life's failures are people who did not realize how close they were to success when they gave up."
—*Thomas A. Edison*

"To invent, you need a good imagination and a pile of junk."
—*Thomas A. Edison*
[A "pile of junk" means a lot of failures.]

A story from Edison's experience illustrates his resilient attitude even in the face of challenges. In December 1914 Edison had worked for 10 years on a storage battery. This had greatly strained his finances. One particular evening spontaneous combustion had broken out in the film room. Within minutes all the packing compounds, celluloid for records and film, and other flammable goods were in flames. Everything was destroyed. Edison was 67.

Although the damage exceeded two million dollars, the buildings were only insured for $238,000. Was Edison's spirit broken to the point of giving up?

The inventor's 24-year-old son, Charles, searched frantically for his father. He finally found him, calmly watching the fire, his face glowing in the reflection, his white hair blowing in the wind. "My heart ached for him," said Charles. "He was 67—no longer a young man—and everything was going up in flames. When he saw me, he shouted, 'Charles, where's your mother?' When I told him I didn't know, he said, 'Find her. Bring her here. She will never see anything like this as long as she lives.' "

The next morning, Edison looked at the ruins and said, "There is great value in disaster. All our mistakes are burned up. Thank God we can start anew." Three weeks after the fire, Edison managed to deliver the first phonograph.[8]

> "I am not discouraged, because every wrong attempt discarded is another step forward."
> — *Thomas A. Edison*

(C) 20TH CENTURY: STEVE JOBS (1955–2011). In our own day, Steve Jobs, the charismatic pioneer and innovative cofounder of Apple Computers, comes to mind when we think of success coming out of failures.

Steve Jobs was born out of wedlock—to an interracial couple. He was put up for adoption. He dropped out of college after only six months. He was fired from the company he founded. And yet he changed the world. Though he died on October 5, 2011, he still lives on in the lives of millions around the world.

Three Apples. It is said there were three apples that changed the world: Eve's, Newton's, and now Jobs'. Of these, we're more familiar with the last one. The very name of his company, Apple—with its rounded, apple fruit logo—seems to say you cannot resist taking a bite.

Steve was only 21 when he started Apple—officially formed on April Fools' Day, 1976. He was forced out in 1985 but returned 15 years later and rescued Apple from near bankruptcy. Two months before his death, in

August of 2011, he had turned the company into the most valuable company in the world.

iJobs. Without doubt, Steve Jobs was one of the greatest geniuses of our time. During his lifetime, he transformed the letter "i" into the most important alphabet character of the day. His technological product lines included the iMac, iTunes, iPod, iPad, iPhone, and, shortly before his death, the iCloud to store our data "in the clouds." At his death, someone quipped about this "icon" of our generation:

> "Steve Jobs didn't die. He went to Heaven to set up iCloud."[9]

iQuotes. There have been many inventors in history, but Jobs seems to exceed them all. In reflecting on Steve Jobs' life and death, it is worth pondering over his own reflections on life. The following classic quotes are excerpted from his 2005 commencement speech at Stanford University. They reveal that sometimes success can result from failure[10]:

> "Getting fired from Apple was the best thing that could have ever happened to me. The heaviness of being successful was replaced by the lightness of being a beginner again, less sure about everything. It freed me to enter one of the most creative periods of my life."

> "Sometimes life hits you in the head with a brick. Don't lose faith. I'm convinced that the only thing that kept me going was that I loved what I did. You've got to find what you love. And that is as true for your work as it is for your lovers. Your work is going to fill a large part of your life, and the only way to be truly satisfied is to do what you believe is great work. And the only way to do great work is to love what you do. If you haven't found it yet, keep looking. Don't settle. As with all matters of the heart, you'll know when you find it. And, like any great relationship, it just gets better and better as the years roll on. So keep looking until you find it. Don't settle."

Be crazy enough to believe with Steve Jobs that even people considered by the world as misfits or failures can actually change the world. I'm alluding here to the original Apple "Think Different" commercial in which

Steve Jobs says:

> "Here's to the crazy ones. The misfits. The rebels. The troublemakers. The round pegs in the square holes. The ones who see things differently. They're not fond of rules. And they have no respect for the status quo. You can quote them, disagree with them, glorify or vilify them. About the only thing you can't do is ignore them. Because they change things. They push the human race forward. And while some may see them as the crazy ones, we see genius. Because the people who are crazy enough to think they can change the world, are the ones who do."[11]

We've looked at three individuals, one each from the 18th, 19th, and 20th centuries, who failed many times and yet eventually succeeded. If, in the 21st century, you also are to succeed through your failures, you must, like Steve Jobs, be crazy enough to believe that misfits or failures can actually change the world. And you very well may. For failure can be the road to success.

> BE CRAZY ENOUGH TO BELIEVE THAT
> MISFITS OR FAILURES CAN
> ACTUALLY CHANGE THE WORLD.
> AND YOU VERY WELL MAY.

4. Develop a Positive Attitude/Disposition Towards Failure

We have said that to succeed through failure, we need to (a) have a different perspective on failure, (b) recognize that you're not alone in the experience of failure, and (c) believe that failure can lead to success. These ways of looking at things should lead us to develop a positive attitude or disposition towards failure.

Consider the following quotes that reveal some healthy dispositions or attitudes on failure.

"One who makes no mistakes never makes anything."
—*Author Unknown*

"A person who never made a mistake never tried anything new."
—*Albert Einstein*

"The men who try to do something and fail are infinitely better than those who try to do nothing and succeed."
—*Lloyd Jones*

Or as my mother would say,

"You cannot eat an egg without breaking the shell." [Meaning those who succeed in life (eat eggs) also break shells (often fail).]

"Failures are the rain droplets through which rainbows appear."
—*SKP*

What these mean is that we need to adopt some particular attitudes. Here are some things to consider.

5. Be Thankful for Failure

Somewhere in the Bible we're told not to worry, but that "in everything" we are to give thanks to the Lord (my paraphrase of PHILIPPIANS 4:6, 7).

What this means is that when you meet sorrow, pain, defeat, or *failure* by the roadside, stop these "friends" and say to them, "Thank you very much. Because of your gifts to me, I'm a better person."

I've explained this attitude in a thought nugget I wrote (titled "Fortunes of Misfortunes"). The relevant sentences in that "Songs in the Dark" thought nugget are these:

　　⌐ EMBEDDED IN THE WORD "MISFORTUNE" IS THE WORD
　　"FORTUNE": FORTUNE MISSED.

　　⌐ MISFORTUNES ARE THE FORTUNES MISSED BY THE PROUD,
　　CARELESS, AND UNGRATEFUL.

⌐ TOMORROW'S FORTUNES ARE ENVELOPED IN TODAY'S MISFORTUNES
LET'S REDEEM THIS HIDDEN WEALTH BY DEVELOPING ATTITUDES OF
GRATITUDE FOR LIFE'S VICISSITUDES.

So, you need to be thankful for failures. Embedded in every failure are the seeds of success. What the 19th-century Scottish preacher George MacDonald (1824–1905) wrote about sorrow equally applies to failure. He said:

"No words can express how much the world owes to sorrow. Most of the Psalms were born in a wilderness. Most of the Epistles were written in prison. The greatest thoughts of the greatest thinkers have all passed through fire. The greatest poets have 'learned in suffering what they taught in song.'... Take comfort, afflicted Christian! When God is about to make preeminent use of a person, He puts him in the fire."

We must be thankful for the many advantages that failure affords us. Someone has summarized:

Failure often softens hearts, develops maturity, broadens thinking, offers insights, prompts innovation, reveals ability, inspires, reinforces the need for risk, builds courage, fortifies, opens other opportunities, brings unexpected benefits, pushes the envelope of future performance, liberates, makes success sweeter, and is preferable to bitterness and regret.[12]
—*Eurice Ed C. Mangaoang*

When God is about to make a person succeed, He allows him or her to go through the sorrow of failure. Therefore be thankful for failure. Gratitude is an attitude that encourages success through failure.

6. Avoid Self-Pity

Another important attitude to adopt in the face of failure is avoiding self-pity. Because there are always consequences to failure, failure can be very painful, humiliating, even shameful. These painful consequences can lead us to self-pity, and ultimately ruin our chances of succeeding through the failures.

Although we may be healed of our wounds—our self-inflicted wounds of sin—yet the consequences of our failures will still remain. There is always fallout from our falls and failures. And the fallout can be painful.

Adam and Eve were forgiven their sin of eating the forbidden fruit, yet their sin unleashed a horrendous fallout of evil and destruction into the whole world. Abraham was forgiven for his lack of faith when he took Hagar as a second wife. But the consequences of his polygamous relationship is still with us to this very day in the wars in the Middle East. David was forgiven his sins of adultery and murder, but it didn't prevent the loss of his four children, a broken and dysfunctional family, and much bloodshed in his nation. Lot—righteous Lot—the man who pitched his tent toward Sodom, was forgiven for his selfishness. Yet, the consequences were incalculable (SEE GENESIS 19).

> SELF-PITY CANNOT SUCCEED THROUGH FAILURE, FOR IT BLINDLY REFUSES TO ACCEPT ITS MISTAKES. IT IS CONTENT WITH FAILURE, CLAMORING FOR ATTENTION BECAUSE IT HAS FAILED.

What is true of our spiritual failures may be equally true of all other failures. There are consequences to failures, whether minor- or mega-consequences. Depending on the nature of the consequences, the cost, pain, shame, and hurt, can lead us to self-pity. But we must be careful not to allow ourselves to wallow in the destructive pit of self-pity. For doing so can ruin our chances of success.

"Self-pity is a death that has no resurrection, a sinkhole from which no rescuing hand can drag you because you have chosen to sink."
—*Elizabeth Elliot*

"Self-pity is easily the most destructive of the nonpharmaceutical narcotics; it is addictive, gives momentary pleasure and separates the victim from reality."
—*John Gardner*

"Self-pity is one of the most dangerous forms of self-centeredness. It fogs our vision."
—*Anonymous*

Indeed, self-pity is never a winning formula. It is a prideful attitude that dooms one's prospect of ever succeeding. Another "Songs in the Dark" thought nugget I wrote to emphasize this point is:

"One doesn't have to be good-looking, talented, intelligent, power-ful, or rich to be proud. Pride also infects some of the ugliest, seeming-ly ungifted, ignorant, oppressed, and poorest people. SELF-PITY is the pride of the weak and suffering. It's the most subtle form of pride because, while pretending to be very needy, it is actually unrenewed self clamoring for attention. Priding itself in its deprived status, self-pity often masquerades as "humility." It's delusional, seeing itself as a "victim" for its own failures and mistakes. When self-pity refuses to acknowledge its loathsome condition, it is incurable and deadly."

Self-pity cannot succeed through failure, for it blindly refuses to accept its mistakes. It is content with failure, clamoring for attention because it has failed.

"My great concern is not whether you have failed, but whether you are content with your failure."
—*Abraham Lincoln*

Instead of self-pity, let's take ownership of our failures, eschewing the kind of attention we try to draw to ourselves because of our misfortunes. We must not try to cover up, deny, excuse, or blame or accuse others for our failures. Neither must we attempt to deal with our mistakes by hiding them under the rug.

We must quit the blame game. Ever since the Fall of Adam and Eve, everyone wants to blame someone else. Adam said, "The woman made me do it." The woman said, "The serpent made me do it." And I'm sure the serpent also, had it been asked about what happened, would have said something along the lines of "God made me do it by creating me that way."

Since the Fall in the Garden of Eden, blaming others for our actions has become the default setting for our responses to our failures. We have become experts in excuses. Everyone is a "victim" or has been "abused." I'm not trivializing the really bad instances to which myriads of people have been subjected. I'm simply challenging the prideful attitude that refuses to recognize that we are responsible for most of our actions—the kind of attitude that leads us to clamor for attention in self-pity.

We will succeed through failure if we take full responsibility for our choices and actions, and allow the Lord to work through the painful consequences.

If it is a spiritual failure, the way out is to acknowledge our sin, repent, confess, and willingly accept the inevitable consequences, trusting that God will forgive you, cleanse you, and restore you.

Here's something to do when we fail—another one of my "Songs in the Dark" thought nuggets. Note the prescription given in the italicized phrases:

"We learn almost nothing in victory; but we learn much in defeat," a football coach once said. I agree. For, when we take time to learn from our mistakes, success has no choice but to fall flat at the feet of failure. Let's give success no choice. How? *Graciously* accept your defeat; *humbly* admit your failures; *courteously* offer no excuses for your faults; *willingly* accept the consequences of your mistakes; *ardently* learn from your missteps; and *fully* surrender your hopes to God's will. Success wins by falling at the feet of failure."

7. Believe That You'll Pull Through the Failure

"Never confuse a single defeat with a final defeat."
—*F. Scott Fitzgerald*

Failure doesn't have to be the end of your life. Think of it as the first step to success. You can pull through your failure—any kind of failure. Even the worst form of failure—the failure of health or life, resulting in death—is never the end. As I said in another one of my weekly "Songs in the Dark" thought nuggets, reflecting on certain passages in Scripture[13]:

> Nations "rise and fall," but the saints "fall and rise"! All other human beings first "live and die," but Jesus "died and lives." It's all a matter of sequence. The fulcrum is He Who was born for the "falling and rising of many."

In the context of my own failure, I have made up my mind that I will allow the Lord to transform my failure into success. This is an attitude of hope. *We must fail our way into success.* For this to happen, God must be factored into our lives. It is He Who can give us a new start. That's why Jesus came. He was born for the "falling and rising of many." (LUKE 1:34)

That God will pull us through our failures is thus stated by David in the book of Psalms:

> The steps of a good man are ordered by the Lord, And He delights in his way. *Though he fall, he shall not be utterly cast down; For the Lord upholds him with His hand.* (PSALM 37:23, 24)

God upholds the righteous with His hand. This is why "though he falls, he is not utterly cast down." In fact, King Solomon said something similar:

> "For a righteous man may fall seven times and rise again, but the wicked shall fall by calamity." (PROVERBS 24:16)

And the prophet Micah adds:

> "Do not rejoice over me, my enemy; *when I fall, I will arise;* when I sit in darkness, the Lord will be a light to me." (MICAH 7:8)

In chapter four of this book, I will employ these scriptural passages and others to develop the "six more chances" mindset to failure—the idea that we must never give up or quit. For now, it is important only to note that failure does not have the final word.

A winning attitude to transform failure into success is a belief that, connected with God, He can pull you through the failure. Faith in God is able to and will give hope in difficult times of failure.

> "THERE CAN BE NO TRIUMPH UNLESS THERE IS A TRIAL. THERE CAN BE NO TESTIMONY UNLESS THERE IS A TEST. THERE CAN BE NO CONQUEST UNLESS THERE IS A CONFLICT."

8. Believe That God Can Give You a Fresh Start

The reason failure is hard to accept is that we feel that the situation is hopeless. But may I remind you that however bad the failures of yesterday are, God can give us a fresh start—by fixing the past. In yet another one of my "Songs in the Dark" thought nuggets, I refer to God's ability to fix the past as His work in giving us "a brand-new yesterday."

We are accustomed to hearing about a "brand-new today" or "brand-new tomorrow." Seldom do we think of a "brand-new yesterday." But God can give us a brand-new yesterday so that we can start anew. I base my understanding upon my reflection on two Scriptural passages: Hebrews 13:8 ("Jesus Christ is the same yesterday, today, and forever"); and 2 Corinthians 5:17 ("If anyone be in Christ, he is a new creation; behold the former things are passed away"). This is what I said on "a brand-new yesterday":

> "Yesterday is the foundation upon which we build houses of today and tomorrow. Though we're able to reside in the homes of today's challenges and those of tomorrow's unknowns, often we're unable to live with yesterday's regrets. Yesterday represents spilled-milk experiences— lost opportunities, costly mistakes, shipwrecked relationships, lost innocence, and ineffaceable records. But Someone can literally step out of

time, journey to our bygone years, and fix yesterday's broken hopes. Jesus Christ is the same YESTERDAY, today, and forever. He alone can give us a brand-new yesterday to enable us build our mansions."

The key to a fresh start, a brand-new yesterday, is Jesus Christ. If you have Him in your life, He will help you start anew and enable you to experience an abundant life (JOHN 10:10).

9. Determine to Have Good Come Out of the Failure

Incredible as it may seem to us, God can actually bring good out of failure, defeat, or mistakes. Therefore, we must determine or work to ensure that something good comes out of it. This fact is captured in a Latin quote with two rhymed words: *Angusta* (from which we get our English word "anguish") and *Augusta* (from which we get the word "august" [i.e., impressive or eminent]). The Latin quote states:

> "Per ANGUSTA ad AUGUSTA"
> It means "Through trials to triumph."

Through anguish we become eminent or august. The Latin quote captures Michael Youssef's insightful words:

> "There can be no triumph unless there is a trial. There can be no testimony unless there is a test. There can be no conquest unless there is a conflict."
> — *Michael Youssef*

Notice that the word "trial" is hidden in the word "triumph"; "test" is embedded in "testimony," and "conflict" is concealed in "conquest." The point is, expect something positive to come out of the seemingly negative experience of failure. This hope is also summed up in my "ANGUSTA ad AUGUSTA" thought nugget:

> To those who are currently going through some dark moments, remember that it is only through ANGUSTA that we get to AUGUSTA. No cross, no crown. Your trials are precious gifts. Treasure them![14]

Joseph might have thought that his plans for the future—his great dreams of future preeminence—had failed when he was rejected and betrayed by his brothers, sold into slavery, wrongfully imprisoned, and forgotten by a fellow prisoner he had helped. And yet, later he was able to say to those who had hurt him, "You meant evil against me; but God meant it for good" (GENESIS 50:20).

Even the "thorns in the flesh," as the apostle Paul described his personal trials and afflictions (1 CORINTHIANS 12:7–10), will work for our good. Paul does not complain, "If I hadn't had this thorn, life would have been wonderful." No, no one has a perfect set of circumstances. Whatever God allows in our pathways are opportunities for advancement.

Beethoven composed much of his music while deaf. Milton composed poetry while blind. Jackie Joyner Kersey won Olympic gold medals after overcoming polio. Florence Nightingale reorganized the hospitals of England while too ill to move from her bed.

The apostle Paul was able to accomplish much, despite his thorn. He built more churches, traveled more distances, and wrote more books than any of the other apostles—despite his many afflictions. He summarizes for us the kinds of trials he faced:

"In stripes above measure, in prisons more frequent, in deaths oft. Of the Jews five times received I forty stripes save one. Thrice was I beaten with rods, once was I stoned, thrice I suffered shipwreck, a night and a day I have been in the deep; in journeyings often, in perils of waters, in perils of robbers, in perils by mine own countrymen, in perils by the heathen, in perils in the city, in perils in the wilderness, in perils in the sea, in perils among false brethren; in weariness and painfulness, in watchings often, in hunger and thirst, in fastings often, in cold and nakedness. Beside those things that are without, that which cometh upon me daily, the care of all the churches" (2 CORINTHIANS 11:23–28).

The lives of Joseph, Paul, and others confirm that, indeed, God can transform our trials and seeming failures for good when they are patiently endured. Even though Satan seeks to use our trials and failures to weaken our will and destroy our commitment to God, the Lord will employ those very things for our good. He will also give us sufficient grace to go through them. The grace by which we are saved is the grace that sustains us even when we encounter trials or failures in our lives.

If time were to have been allowed me, I'd have illustrated from the Bible how God often brought good out of failures. But the greatest example of God bringing good out of evil is the failure of Adam and Eve—the first-family eagles. (I'm using the word "eagle" as a symbol for those who choose to live to their highest God-given potential).

> THE GRACE BY WHICH WE ARE SAVED IS THE GRACE THAT SUSTAINS US EVEN WHEN WE ENCOUNTER TRIALS OR FAILURES IN OUR LIVES.

Adam and Eve were the first wounded eagles. Their wounds were also self-inflicted because they consciously chose to disobey God. As a consequence, suffering, pain, evil, and death were introduced into this world.

But it should be noted that, like every other sin, Satan was the one who tripped our first parents into sin when they ventured onto the forbidden ground. Satan attacked the first eagle couple because of his hatred for God. The enemy hated God so deeply that, unable to attack God Himself, he chose to attack the holy pair created in the image of God. Satan knew Adam and Eve were the objects of God's supreme love, thus by attacking them he was attacking God Himself.

The ultimate aim of Satan in causing the wounding of Adam and Eve was to effect humanity's *eternal separation from God*. After all, sin creates a barrier between God and us (ISAIAH 59). Thus, when Satan succeeded in wounding the First Eagle Couple, he thought that was it: eternal separation from God. Humanity would be forever cut off from God.

But what was meant to cause eternal separation between God and humanity became the occasion for which *God became eternally bound* to humanity. How?

First, through Christ's incarnation, God became human, and throughout all eternity would identify with humanity. *Divinity* is eternally bound to humanity. Christ's name "Emmanuel" means "God with us." Instead of eternal separation, now we have an eternal bond. God with us. God is represented among His created beings.

Second, after Christ's death, resurrection, and ascension, He carried with Him to Heaven His *human* frame, even bearing its scars in His hands, feet, and side. Since Christ is also God, the implication is that by bearing our human frame in Heaven, humanity would be forever represented in the Godhead, in the Trinity! Of the three Members of the Godhead, one of Them is also human. Humanity alone, not even angels or some other higher order of created beings, is represented in the Trinity. Christ, the Most Wounded Eagle, Who had always been God, will forever represent fallen yet restored humanity. He will forever identify with us.

Think of it as good coming out of evil: One of the Members of the Trinity bears a human frame! In this way, *humanity* is eternally bound to Divinity. In the words of E. G. White, "Heaven is enshrined in humanity, and humanity is enfolded in the bosom of Infinite Love" (DESIRE OF AGES, P. 26).

Third, our wayward planet Earth, which on account of sin was claimed by Satan as his own, will become the seat of God's throne forever. This planet Earth, the original home of Adam and Eve, but which became the place of Christ's shame, humiliation, and agonizing death on Calvary, will forever be the capital of God's government:

> And I saw the Holy City, the New Jerusalem, coming down from God out of Heaven like a bride beautifully dressed for her husband. I heard a loud shout from the throne, saying, "Look, God's home is now among His people! He will live with them, and they will be His people. God Himself will be with them. He will wipe

every tear from their eyes, and there will be no more death or sorrow or crying or pain. All these things are gone forever (REVELATION 21:2–4).

Talk about something good coming out of failure! Sin—the wounding of Adam and Eve, and that of the Most Wounded Eagle—would become the means by which we see the glory of God—more than if there had been no sin.

In other words, our individual salvation is by no means the only reason for Christ's incarnation and death on Calvary. By it Christ has both revealed infinite love to the universe and intends to perpetuate His infinite providence by using this once dark earth as the center for forever revealing His glorious light. Indeed, John 3:16 is about much more than God giving Christ to die for us. No, He simply gave Him to us. Instead of an eternal separation from God because of sin, God found a way to bring about an eternal bond.

These thoughts are beautifully couched in three pregnant paragraphs in Ellen G. White's *Desire of Ages*, pages 25–26. This book, in my opinion, is the best devotional commentary on the life of Christ.

In practical terms, what this means is that despite your own failure, your own "self-inflicted" wounds, if you allow the Lord to have His way in your life, He can bring good out of a messy, seemingly intractable situation.

Indeed, I can personally testify that despite the pain and shame of my own self-inflicted wounds, I am beginning to see some good coming out of this evil. My own repentance and relationship with Christ have been deepened. I've gained a greater appreciation for the love and justice of God. I have greater empathy for people who are struggling. My reading of the Bible has been enriched, seeing God's amazing grace ceaselessly working amidst His discipline and judgment of His children. The privilege of talking about my failure in a manner that leads others to Christ. And many more.

Also, judging from lives that have already been impacted and changed by their reading of my reflections on my personal failure, I can already see God turning into good what the enemy meant for evil.

Let's Recap: Let me now recap the nine points I've made thus far regarding how we can allow God to bring success out of our failures:

⌐ 1. HAVE A DIFFERENT PERSPECTIVE ON FAILURE

⌐ 2. RECOGNIZE THAT YOU'RE NOT ALONE

⌐ 3. BELIEVE THAT FAILURE CAN LEAD TO SUCCESS

⌐ 4. DEVELOP A POSITIVE ATTITUDE TOWARDS FAILURE

⌐ 5. BE THANKFUL FOR FAILURE

⌐ 6. AVOID SELF-PITY

⌐ 7. BELIEVE THAT YOU'LL PULL THROUGH THE FAILURE
[this is an issue of *Hope*]

⌐ 8. BELIEVE THAT GOD CAN GIVE YOU A FRESH START
[He can give you a brand-new yesterday]

⌐ 9. DETERMINE TO HAVE GOOD COME OUT OF THE FAILURE

Let me now make my last point. I love to end on the number ten because it reminds me of the Ten Commandments: the perfect standard of success—both spiritual success and success in our education, profession, marriage, etc.

10. Get Up Immediately and Keep Going From Failure to Success

"Our greatest weakness lies in giving up. The most certain way to succeed is to try just one more time."
—*Thomas A. Edison*

As soon as you fail, get up immediately. Don't waste time on the floor. Get up, brush off the dirt, and keep going. And the best time to get started is today. Tomorrow will be too late. Today is the day. As I explained in another one of my "Songs in the Dark" thought nuggets,

"Today is the last day of yesterday and the first day of tomorrow. It's the conclusion to yesterday's chapter and the introduction to your new book. Why dwell on a written past, when you can write the future today?"[15]

Immediately shake off the failure, step up, and keep going.

> LIFE IS GOING TO SHOVEL
> DIRT ON YOU, ALL KINDS OF DIRT.
> DON'T LET IT BURY YOU.
> SHAKE IT OFF AND STEP UP.

Parable of the Old Donkey: A parable is told of a farmer who owned an old donkey that fell into the farmer's abandoned well one morning. The farmer heard the animal braying desperately from its hopeless position, battered and bruised. The donkey cried piteously for hours, looking upward for a savior.

The farmer sympathized with the donkey. But after carefully assessing the situation, he felt that the animal was quite old and the well needed to be covered up anyway; so it just wasn't worth the trouble trying to retrieve the donkey.

So he called his neighbors together and told them what had happened and enlisted them to help haul dirt to bury the old donkey in the well and put him out of his misery. Each of his neighbors grabbed a shovel and began to shovel dirt into the well. Realizing what was happening, the donkey at first cried and wailed horribly.

But as the farmer and his neighbors continued shoveling, and the dirt hit his back, a thought struck the donkey. It suddenly dawned on him that every time a shovel load of dirt landed on his back, he should simply *shake it off and step up!*

And so he did, blow after blow. "Shake it off and step up ... shake it off and step up ... shake it off and step up!" he repeated to encourage himself as the well grew shorter and the light above grew brighter.

No matter how painful the blows, or distressing the situation seemed, the old donkey fought "panic" and just kept right on *shaking it off and stepping up!*

It wasn't long before the old donkey, battered and exhausted, stepped triumphantly over the wall of that well as the neighbors and a farmer once intent on burying him learned a lesson about overcoming adversity in their own lives: SHAKE IT OFF AND STEP UP!

Life is going to shovel dirt on you, all kinds of dirt. The trick to getting out of the well is to not let it bury you, *but to shake it off and take a step up.* Each of our troubles or setbacks is a stepping-stone. As I've told the young people I've trained and empowered over the years,

"Setbacks shouldn't set you back. They are stepping-stones. Step on the stones and you'll move upward and forward."

"Make discouragement your encouragement."

It is the same idea captured in the book *Messages to Young People* by Ellen G. White:

"Opposing circumstances should create a firm determination to overcome them. The breaking down of one barrier will give greater ability and courage to go forward. Press with determination in the right direction, and *circumstances will be your helpers, not your hindrances*" (*MESSAGES TO YOUNG PEOPLE*, 99, 100; EMPHASIS MINE).

When you face opposing circumstances, those challenges should make you more determined to overcome them. Because when you overcome one barrier, it will give you additional ability and courage to go forward. "Press with determination." That is another way of saying Shake it off and step up! Keep going on. Never give up.

III. WHO IS A FAILURE?

Before addressing the final question, "Who is a failure?" let me reiterate three simple things we need to do in order to succeed through failure: (1) Have a different perspective on failure, (2) Adopt a positive attitude towards failure, and (3) Have an abiding connection with God as a key Partner in your struggles with failure.

Everything I've said thus far can be summed up in those three points. Here, now, are some final thoughts:

"Fall seven times, stand up eight."
—*Japanese proverb*

"Our greatest glory is not in never falling, but in rising every time we fall."
—*Confucius*

"Defeat is not the worst of failures. Not to have tried is the true failure."
—*George E. Woodberry*

"You always pass failure on the way to success."
——*Mickey Rooney*

"Try and fail, but don't fail to try."
—*Stephen Kaggwa*

"We must not be afraid to break the egg shell
if we want to eat the egg."
—*African mother's proverb [my mum]*

"Stumbling is not falling."
—*Portuguese proverb*

"I didn't fail the test, I just found 100 ways to do it wrong."
—*Benjamin Franklin*

"I look at failure as education. In that respect I'm very well educated."
—*Kathy Ireland*

"A life spent making mistakes is not only more honorable but more useful than a life spent in doing nothing."
—*George Bernard Shaw*

"There is no such thing as failure. It is just a temporary postponement of success."
—*Buddy Ebsen*

"If you know you are going to fail, then fail gloriously!"
—*Cate Blanchett*

Anytime you're about to give up because of failure, think about the following examples that were forwarded to me by a student several years ago:

- NOAH WAS A DRUNK.
- ABRAHAM WAS TOO OLD.
- ISAAC WAS A DAYDREAMER.
- JACOB WAS A LIAR.
- LEAH WAS UGLY.
- JOSEPH WAS ABUSED.
- MOSES HAD A STUTTERING PROBLEM.
- GIDEON WAS AFRAID.
- SAMSON HAD LONG HAIR AND WAS A WOMANIZER.
- RAHAB WAS A PROSTITUTE.
- JEREMIAH AND TIMOTHY WERE TOO YOUNG.
- DAVID HAD AN AFFAIR AND WAS A MURDERER.
- ELIJAH WAS SUICIDAL.
- ISAIAH PREACHED NAKED
  [well, probably half clad, wearing only his inner garments].
- JONAH RAN FROM GOD.
- NAOMI WAS A WIDOW.
- JOB WENT BANKRUPT.
- PETER DENIED CHRIST.
- THE DISCIPLES FELL ASLEEP WHILE PRAYING.
- MARTHA WORRIED ABOUT EVERYTHING.
- THE SAMARITAN WOMAN WAS DIVORCED, MORE THAN ONCE.

⌣ ZACCHAEUS WAS TOO SMALL.

⌣ PAUL WAS TOO RELIGIOUS . . . *and*

⌣ LAZARUS WAS DEAD.

All of the above individuals failed at some point in their lives. But the Lord enabled them to succeed through failure. He can do the same for you in life. In case you're still wondering "Who is a failure?" listen to these words:

"Defeat doesn't finish a man—quit[ting] does. A man is not finished when he's defeated. He's finished when he quits."
—*Richard M. Nixon*

"The only true failure lies in failure to start."
—*Harold Blake Walker*

"A failure is a man who has blundered, but is not able to cash in on the experience."
—*Elbert Hubbard*

"My great concern is not whether you have failed, but whether you are content with your failure."
—*Abraham Lincoln*

"Life's real failure is when you do not realize how close you were to success when you gave up."
—*Anonymous*

"A man may fall many times, but he won't be a failure until he says that someone pushed him."
—*Elmer G. Letterman*

"There is no failure except in no longer trying."
—*Elbert Hubbard*

"You never fail until you stop trying."
—*Albert Einstein*

"The people who try to do something and fail are infinitely better than those who try to do nothing and succeed."
—*Lloyd James*

> SUCCESS THROUGH FAILURE IS WHAT THE GOSPEL IS ALL ABOUT: SALVATION FROM THE FAILURES OF SIN. IT IS THE REASON JESUS CAME TO DIE FOR OUR SINS.

Giselle, it is stroke of wisdom and of your spiritual maturity that even as we celebrate your success you've chosen to remind us that failures will also come in life, and consequently we must learn how to get back on track. I've shared a few thoughts with you—thoughts that have been refracted through the prism of my own recent failure. I trust that the thoughts will come handy to you as you journey through life:

1. HAVE A DIFFERENT PERSPECTIVE ON FAILURE

2. RECOGNIZE THAT YOU'RE NOT ALONE

3. BELIEVE THAT FAILURE CAN LEAD TO SUCCESS

4. DEVELOP A POSITIVE ATTITUDE TOWARDS FAILURE

5. BE THANKFUL FOR FAILURE

6. AVOID SELF-PITY

7. BELIEVE THAT YOU'LL PULL THROUGH THE FAILURE
[this is an issue of *hope*]

8. BELIEVE THAT GOD CAN GIVE YOU A FRESH START
[He can give you a brand-new yesterday]

9. DETERMINE TO HAVE GOOD COME OUT OF THE FAILURE

10. GET UP IMMEDIATELY AND KEEP GOING FROM FAILURE TO SUCCESS

The Gospel of Jesus Christ: The Answer to Failure

Success through failure is what the Gospel is all about: salvation from the failures of sin. It is the reason Jesus came to die for our sins. The salvation He brought is actually the excellence or success we seek in all facets of life: academic, professional, personal, and spiritual. Though He Himself never once failed, for our sake He became a "failure"—according to the world's measure of success.[16]

No better words can describe Him than those of James Allen Francis, in his famous 1926 essay titled *One Solitary Life*:[17]

He was born in an obscure village,
    the Child of a peasant woman.
He grew up in another obscure village, where
He worked in a carpenter's shop until He was thirty.
    Then for three years He was an itinerant preacher.
He never owned a home.
He never wrote a book.
He never held an office.
He never had a family.
He never went to college.
He never visited a big city.
He never traveled more than two hundred miles from the place
    where He was born.
He never did one of the things that accompanies greatness.
He had no credentials but Himself.
He was only thirty-three when the tide of public opinion
    turned against Him.
One of His friends betrayed Him.
Others deserted Him.
One of them denied Him.
He was turned over to His enemies, and
He went through the mockery of a trial.
He was nailed upon a cross between two thieves.
While dying, His executioners gambled for His clothing,
    the only property He had on Earth.
When dead, He was laid in a borrowed grave

through the pity of a friend.
But three days later He rose from the dead.
Those are the facts of His human life.
Twenty centuries have come and gone,
And today He is the Centerpiece of the human race
And the Leader of mankind's progress.
All the armies that have ever marched,
All the navies that have ever sailed,
All the parliaments that have ever sat, and
All the kings that have ever reigned, put together,
Have not affected the life of mankind on this earth
As powerfully as that One Solitary Life.

Indeed, when measured by the way most of us measure success, His earthly life would have been deemed a failure. And yet, no other person, army, or movement has affected the people of this earth as much as the *One Solitary Life* of our Lord Jesus Christ. Through Him God has provided salvation (true excellence or success in all facets of life) to all who are struggling with the failures of sin. And, in the words of E. G. White, "life with Him is no failure."[18]

The success the Lord wants to see in our lives involves our obedience and faithfulness to Him, regardless of consequences or personal cost. The Gospel's criteria of success is being loyal to Him in our personal relationship with Him, with others, and in every aspect of life. Failure is when we live our lives without accomplishing His goals and purposes for our lives.

Through Christ, we can actually succeed through failure. We can be victorious because He is "One Who knows no failure":

When we give ourselves wholly to God, and in our work follow His directions, He makes Himself responsible for its accomplishment. He would not have us conjecture as to the success of our honest endeavors. *Not once should we even think of failure. We are to cooperate with One Who knows no failure*" (E. G. WHITE, *CHRIST'S OBJECT LESSONS*, P. 363.1).

Giselle, this is not the day you are hatched or matched or dispatched. Rather, it is the day you are *batched*. You're now officially part of this year's batch of graduating students. But more than that, you are now officially one of Christ's ambassadors to the world.

Though you're graduating today, your lifework will never end. The education will never cease. And, as we are told, apparent failure is part of the training God gives His children for them to succeed—in this life and in the world to come:

> Some God trains by bringing to them disappointment and *apparent failure*. It is His purpose that they shall learn to master difficulties. *He inspires them with a determination to prove every apparent failure a success.* Often men pray and weep because of the perplexities and obstacles that confront them. But if they will hold the beginning of their confidence steadfast unto the end, God will make their way clear. *Success will come as they struggle against apparently insurmountable difficulties and with success will come the greatest joy.* (E. G. WHITE, *GOSPEL WORKERS,* P. 269.2)

> FAILURE IS WHEN WE LIVE
> OUR LIVES WITHOUT ACCOMPLISHING
> GOD'S PURPOSES FOR OUR LIVES.

Giselle, as a lasting tribute to your graduation, and in my capacity as an expert on failure, I've decided TODAY to make this presentation the outline of a future book (and perhaps the seed for other books). Thank you for giving me this honor. I leave with you this Bible promise:

> No man shall be able to stand before you all the days of your life; as I was with Moses, so I will be with you. I will not leave you nor forsake you. Be strong and of good courage, for to this people you shall divide as an inheritance the land which I swore to their fathers to give them. Only be strong and very courageous, that you may observe to do according to

all the law which Moses My servant commanded you; do not turn from it to the right hand or to the left, that you may prosper wherever you go. This Book of the Law shall not depart from your mouth, but you shall meditate in it day and night, that you may observe to do according to all that is written in it. For then you will make your way prosperous, and then you will have good success. Have I not commanded you? Be strong and of good courage; do not be afraid, nor be dismayed, for the Lord your God is with you wherever you go" (JOSHUA 1:5–9).

CHAPTER 2

⁓

TRUE SUCCESS & APPARENT FAILURE

Sources for Knowledge & Models to Emulate
(Inspirational Thoughts From the Past)

A FOUNDATION OF AUTHORITY

History affords many examples and lessons on success and failure. It provides myriads of sources from which to understand what constitutes true success and true failure, and it presents different arguments as to whether or not we are most benefited by learning from success or from failure.

In times of failure—whether personal, professional, or spiritual—one needs to be very sure of one's foundation of authority, lest one sinks deeper into despair and even commits suicide. Depending on the credibility of one's ultimate authority, the arguments from history may be compelling, confusing, or contradictory; and the verdict from history on questions about success and failure may be either true or false, helpful or dangerous.

In my search for meaningful answers for recovery from my own spiritual failure, I found only one source to be dependable: the Word of God. The *inspired* Word of God was the only Book that provided trustworthy guidance in my time of need.

> IN TIMES OF FAILURE—WHETHER
> PERSONAL, PROFESSIONAL, OR SPIRITUAL
> —ONE NEEDS TO BE VERY SURE OF ONE'S
> FOUNDATION OF AUTHORITY, LEST ONE
> SINKS DEEPER INTO DESPAIR AND
> EVEN COMMITS SUICIDE.

This inspired Word, or the Holy Scriptures, revealed to me the *living Word*, the Lord Jesus Christ, Who alone never failed and Who has made ample provision for everyone that has experienced failure. He says to all who have failed in life: "Come to Me, all of you who are weary and carry heavy burdens, and I will give you rest" (MATTHEW 11:28, NLT).

Restating the above fact, in the manner in which I typically begin my Bible lectures to students and other audiences,

> "The Bible is the inspired Word of God. It is the only Book that reveals to us compelling answers to questions about success and failure. Let us study the Bible, for if we do so, we shall find rest for our souls."

Searching the Scriptures and meditating upon their messages was the most useful thing that rescued me from discouragement and despair when I experienced my failure. The Bible also became the basis upon which I evaluated conflicting counsels and criticisms, from friends and foes, regarding how I should relate to my failure.

Furthermore, the Word of God was the sole basis upon which I gleaned insights from authors—past and present, secular or godly. And the Scriptures informed my verdict on what I should or shouldn't do when my world crashed on account of my failure. The value of Scriptures is summed up thus:

> "You have been taught the Holy Scriptures from childhood, and they have given you the wisdom to receive the salvation that comes by trusting in Christ Jesus. All Scripture is inspired by God and is useful

to teach us what is true and to make us realize what is wrong in our lives. It corrects us when we are wrong and teaches us to do what is right. God uses it to prepare and equip His people to do every good work" (2 TIMOTHY 3:15–17).

The Scriptures must be the cornerstone on which we build our world-views on every issue of life. Not tradition, not experience, not nature, not history, not psychology, nor any other human source of authority. Only the Word of God, or as our Protestant forebears put it, "The Bible and the Bible only" is our rule of faith. It is our "only creed," to borrow words from the preamble of our fundamental beliefs. In fact, our fundamental belief #1 makes it explicitly clear that we should embrace ideas in any other source if, and only if, the ideas accord with Scripture.[1]

Thus, my views and attitude on success and failure, as well as the spiritual nuggets I seek to share in this book from the works of others, have been refracted through the lenses of Scripture. My ultimate goal is that we shall find succinct answers to our questions and triumph through our failures.

A belief in the sole authority of Scriptures does not mean there's no value in the thoughts of non-biblical sources. There is! In fact, in some instances these sources express concepts in ways that are more easily understood than the biblical writers. This is why in the previous chapter (as also in subsequent ones) I have shared quotes and ideas from non-biblical writers, both past and present. And I'm sure there are countless others whose thoughts are unconsciously echoed throughout the pages of this volume.[2]

Charles H. Spurgeon (1834-1892)—the famed English Baptist preacher, author, and editor—aptly explains the importance of drawing upon the insights of others. He wrote:

"The man who never reads will never be read; he who never quotes will never be quoted. He who will not use the thoughts of other men's brains, proves that he has no brains of his own."[3]
—*Charles Spurgeon*

Consequently, in this second section of *Six More Chances* I bring together some spiritual nuggets that explain what constitutes true success and failure. The inspirational thoughts come from the pen of my favorite devotional writer, E. G. White. She lived in the 19th century and was the contemporary of other spiritual giants like Dwight L. Moody, F. B. Meyer, Henry Drummond, R. A. Torrey, Ralph Connor, Charles Spurgeon, and Oswald Chambers.[4]

Through this remarkably gifted Christian author I overcame my fear of failure, embracing failure as an opportunity to learn and grow. But before I share the lessons I learned on true success and apparent failure, allow me to say a word on the fear that often attends failure.

> "THE MAN WHO NEVER READS WILL NEVER BE READ; HE WHO NEVER QUOTES WILL NEVER BE QUOTED. HE WHO WILL NOT USE THE THOUGHTS OF OTHER MEN'S BRAINS, PROVES THAT HE HAS NO BRAINS OF HIS OWN."

THE FEAR OF FAILURE

The fear of failure is the reason why many of us evade responsibilities that lead to success. This fear of failure prevents us from benefiting from the many advantages that can only be learned from such experiences.

Many become inefficient by evading responsibilities for *fear of failure*. Thus they fail of gaining that education which results from experience, and which reading and study and all the advantages otherwise gained, cannot give them.[5]

To succeed in life, we should not allow the circumstances of life—failure included—to have mastery over us. We must rather prevail over them.

Man can shape circumstances, but circumstances should not be allowed to shape the man. We should seize upon circumstances as instruments with which to work. We are to master them, but should not permit them to master us.[6]

The only way we can prevail over the fear of failure is to make God a priority in every aspect of our lives:

If you would secure the grand aim and purpose of life without mistake in your choice or *fear of failure*, you must make God first and last and best in every plan and work and thought.[7]

In her numerous works, E. G. White has spoken volumes on how to succeed in every aspect of life: academic, business, family, leadership, health, spirituality, and many others. She has also spoken about how we can transform apparent failure into success.

I. TRUE SUCCESS

To achieve true success we need to look at the spiritual and practical components of success. We need to recognize the connection between our efforts and our reliance upon divine power.

Success is not the result of chance or of destiny; it is the outworking of God's own providence, the reward of faith and discretion, of virtue and persevering effort.[8]

The elements of character that make a man successful and honored among men—the irrepressible desire for some greater good, the indomitable will, the strenuous exertion, the untiring perseverance—are not to be crushed out.[9]

There is such a thing as true and false success, the former referring to the divine perspective and the latter describing how the world looks at success. The following nuggets from our 19th-century devotional author detail some key elements of true success (italics my own):

1. TRUE SUCCESS IS OF DIVINE ORIGIN

True success is dependent on the One Who has said, "Without Me ye can do nothing" (JOHN 15:5).[10]

Remember that *true success* comes from God alone, and that every particle of the praise and glory belongs to Him. We are God's husbandry, God's building.[11]

It is divine power that gives [God's servants] success.[12]

True success is given to men and women by the God Who gave success to Daniel. He Who read the heart of Daniel looked with pleasure upon His servant's purity of motive, his determination to honor the Lord.[13]

2. TRUE SUCCESS DEPENDS ON HUMAN-DIVINE CONNECTION

While God was working in Daniel and his companions "to will and to do of His good pleasure," they were working out their own salvation. (PHILIPPIANS 2:13). Herein is revealed the outworking of the divine principle of cooperation, without which no true success can be attained. Human effort avails nothing without divine power; and without human endeavor, divine effort is with many of no avail. To make God's grace our own, we must act our part. His grace is given to work in us to will and to do, but never as a substitute for our effort.[14]

Human strength is weakness, human wisdom is folly. Our success does not depend on our talents or learning, but on our living connection with God.[15]

True success in any line of work is not the result of chance or accident or destiny. It is the outworking of God's providences, the reward of faith and discretion, of virtue and perseverance. Fine mental qualities and a high moral tone are not the result of accident. God gives opportunities; success depends upon the use made of them.[16]

3. TRUE SUCCESS BEGINS WITH TOTAL SURRENDER TO GOD

When we give ourselves wholly to God and in our work follow His directions, He makes Himself responsible for its accomplishment. He would not have us conjecture as to the success of our honest endeavors. Not once should we even think of failure. We are to cooperate with One Who knows no failure.[17]

That which lies at the foundation of business integrity and of *true success* is the recognition of God's ownership. The Creator of all things, He is the original Proprietor. We are His stewards. All that we have is a trust from Him, to be used according to His direction.[18]

4. TRUE SUCCESS IS THE RESULT OF ENABLEMENT BY THE HOLY SPIRIT

We cannot rightly estimate the value of the gift of the Holy Spirit. Those who yield themselves to the control of this Spirit are made pure and holy. Efficiency in God's work comes not by wading through an immense amount of study, but by a willingness to be guided and controlled by the Spirit. God only can give *true success*. Yoked up with Christ, men will become more precious than gold, even than the golden wedge of Ophir.[19]

It is not the ability of the agent or worker, but it is the Spirit of God moving upon the heart that will give *true success*.[20]

5. TRUE SUCCESS IS ROOTED IN GOD'S WORD

There is no branch of legitimate business for which the Bible does not afford an essential preparation. Its principles of diligence, honesty, thrift, temperance, and purity are the secret of true success. These principles, as set forth in the Book of Proverbs, constitute a treasury of practical wisdom.[21]

God cares for us as intelligent beings, and He has given us His Word as a lamp to our feet and a light to our path. Its teachings have a vital bearing upon our prosperity in all the relations of life. Even in our temporal affairs it will be a wiser guide than any other counselor. Its divine instruction points the only way to *true success*. There is no social position, no phase of human experience, for which the study of the Bible is not an essential preparation.[22]

6. TRUE SUCCESS DEMANDS A DEFINITE AIM OR MINDSET

Success in any line demands a definite aim. He who would achieve true success in life must keep steadily in view the aim worthy of his endeavor.[23]

Success in any line demands a definite aim. If you want to achieve *true success* in life, set goals worthy of your efforts.[24]

When you make up your mind to do something on which your heart is set, you do not give up for difficulties, but try again and again. Put the same energy and determination to succeed in the service of Christ, and you will not fail of a reward.[25]

7. TRUE SUCCESS KEEPS A PERSPECTIVE ON ETERNITY

True success in education, as in everything else, is found in keeping the future life in view ... He who appreciates probationary time as the preparatory school of life will use it to secure to himself a title to the heavenly mansions, a membership in the higher school. For this school the youth are to be educated, disciplined, and trained by forming such characters as God will approve.[26]

8. TRUE SUCCESS ADHERES TO RIGHT PRINCIPLES

The Bible teaches men to act from principle, and whenever we successfully resist evil influence, we are strengthening that principle which has been assailed. The mere possession of talent is no guarantee of usefulness or happiness in life. Right principles are the only basis of *true success*.[27]

It should be written on the conscience as with a pen of iron upon a rock, that no man can achieve *true success* while violating the eternal principles of right.[28]

The Lord sees not as man sees. Those whom He most loves and honors are often the objects of the scorn and derision of the enemy. He desires us to learn the lesson that we shall not gain *true success* in His work by trying to meet the criterion of the world. Hypocrisy and pretense can find no favor in His sight. The victories gained by the soul are not measured by outside appearance or by the praise of men, but by the goodness which shines forth in the life, by the firm adherence to God's holy law.[29]

Christ's method alone will give true success.[30]

9. TRUE SUCCESS REQUIRES A BALANCED LIFESTYLE: HEALTH, ENVIRONMENT & RECREATION

Better than any other inheritance of wealth you can give to your children will be the gift of a healthy body, a sound mind, and a noble character. Those who understand what constitutes life's *true success* will be wise betimes. They will keep in view life's best things in their choice of a home.

Instead of dwelling where only the works of men can be seen, where the sights and sounds frequently suggest thoughts of evil, where turmoil and confusion bring weariness and disquietude, go where you can look upon the works of God. Find rest of spirit in the beauty and quietude and peace of nature. Let the eye rest on the green fields, the groves, and the hills. Look up to the blue sky, unobscured by the city's dust and smoke, and breathe the invigorating air of heaven. Go where, apart from the distractions and dissipations of city life, you can give your children your companionship, where you can teach them to learn of God through His works, and train them for lives of integrity and usefulness.[31]

There is a distinction between recreation and amusement. Recreation, when true to its name, re-creation, tends to strengthen and build up.

Calling us aside from our ordinary cares and occupations, it affords refreshment for mind and body, and thus enables us to return with new vigor to the earnest work of life. Amusement, on the other hand, is sought for the sake of pleasure and is often carried to excess; it absorbs the energies that are required for useful work and thus proves a hindrance to *life's true success.*[32]

10. TRUE SUCCESS DEPENDS UPON THE DISCIPLINE OF THE MIND

Many greatly magnify seeming difficulties and then begin to pity themselves and give way to despondency. Such need to make an entire change in themselves. They *need to discipline themselves* to put forth exertion and to overcome all childish feelings. They should determine that life shall not be spent in working at trifles… Everyone should have an aim, an object, in life. *The loins of the mind should be girded up and the thoughts be trained* to keep to the point, as the compass to the pole. The mind should be directed in the right channel, according to well-formed plans. Then every step will be a step in advance … *Success or failure in this life depends much upon the manner in which the thoughts are disciplined.*[33]

II. APPARENT FAILURE

We're looking briefly at failure because people fail every day and so do companies, institutions, and organizations. However, we often prefer talking about success, especially big successes, even though hardly anyone can claim to have been successful in all their endeavors. Little is said about failure. Everyone knows what it feels like—there is shame, pain, humiliation, and sometimes a note of complete dejection.

But failure is never a dead end, for with God, failure is only apparent. It may appear as failure, but with His help, even the direst situation can be transformed into success. Even spiritual failure doesn't have to disqualify us from rising back to success:

Should they [God's faithful workers] fail in any of their undertakings, they should not therefore be deemed unqualified for the work; for to err is human. They should not become discouraged, but should endeavor to learn by every *apparent failure* how to make a success of the next effort. And if they connect with the Source of wisdom they will surely succeed.[34]

> WITH GOD, FAILURE IS ONLY APPARENT.
> IT MAY APPEAR AS FAILURE, BUT WITH HIS HELP,
> EVEN THE DIREST SITUATION CAN BE
> TRANSFORMED INTO SUCCESS.

We may see the misfortunes of failure as they really are: actually fortunes of success that need to be redeemed. Christ not only helps us turn failures into success, but His own refusal to be discouraged provides an example.

The following spiritual nuggets reveal attitudes toward failure that enable us to succeed through *apparent failures*. They explain how we can view failures.

1. FAILURES AS DISGUISED BLESSINGS

He [Christ] will work through those who can see mercy in misery, and gain in loss. When the Light of the world passes by, privilege will be discerned in hardship, order in confusion, success in *apparent failure*. Calamities will be seen as disguised blessings; woes, as mercies. Laborers from the common people, sharing the sorrows of their fellow men as their Master shared the sorrows of the whole human race, will by faith see Him working with them.[35]

2. FAILURE AS A WAY OF ADVANCEMENT

The worker who knows the meaning of union with Christ ... realizes that he is but an instrument, and that he must be passive in the Master's hands. Trials come to him; for unless thus tested, he would never know his lack of wisdom and experience. But if he seeks the Lord with humility and trust, every trial will work for his good. He may sometimes seem to fail, but his *apparent failure* may be God's way of bringing him true advancement, and may mean a better knowledge of himself and a firmer trust in Heaven. He may still make mistakes, but he learns not to repeat these mistakes. He becomes stronger to resist evil, and others reap benefit from his example.[36]

3. FAILURE AS A WAY TO MASTER DIFFICULTIES

Some God trains by bringing to them disappointment and apparent failure. It is His purpose that they shall learn to master difficulties. He inspires them with a determination to prove every *apparent failure* a success. Often men pray and weep because of the perplexities and obstacles that confront them. But if they will hold the beginning of their confidence steadfast unto the end, God will make their way clear. Success will come as they struggle against apparently insurmountable difficulties and with success will come the greatest joy.[37]

The workers whom He is leading may at times be in great perplexity. It is His plan that many difficulties shall be met and mastered. He inspires the workers with the determination to make every *apparent failure* prove a success. They are determined to walk in the light that is shining on their pathway, and although they encounter many obstacles, yet they declare, "I will not fail or be discouraged."[38]

4. FAILURE AS A WAY TO SUCCESS

They [Christian workers] should not become discouraged, but should endeavor to learn by every *apparent failure* how to make a success of the next effort. And if they connect with the Source of wisdom, they will surely succeed.[39]

We need to look heavenward in faith. We are not to be discouraged because of *apparent failure*, nor should we be disheartened by delay. We should work cheerfully, hopefully, gratefully, believing that the earth holds in her bosom rich treasures for the faithful worker to garner, stores richer than gold or silver. The mountains and hills are changing; the earth is waxing old like a garment; but the blessing of God, which spreads for His people a table in the wilderness, will never cease.[40]

Sometimes He trains His workers by bringing to them disappointment and *apparent failure*. It is His purpose that they shall learn to master difficulties.

Often men are tempted to falter before the perplexities and obstacles that confront them. But if they will hold the beginning of their confidence steadfast unto the end, God will make the way clear. Success will come to them as they struggle against difficulties.[41]

5. FAILURE AS A SURMOUNTABLE REALITY

Christ refused to be discouraged. He armed Himself with the Word of God, and kept His mission constantly before Him. He was undeterred by *apparent failure* because He knew that truth would finally triumph in the contest with evil. We must learn from His example. Writes E. G. White:

As the world's Redeemer, Christ was constantly confronted with *apparent failure*. He, the Messenger of mercy to our world, seemed to do little of the work He longed to do in uplifting and saving. Satanic influences were constantly working to oppose His way. But He would not be discouraged. Through the prophecy of Isaiah He declares,

"*I have labored in vain, I have spent My strength for nought, and in vain: Yet surely My judgment is with the Lord, and My work with My God.*" (ISAIAH 49:4)

Upon this word Jesus rested, and He gave Satan no advantage... With prophetic eye Christ traced the scenes to take place in His last great conflict. He knew that when He should exclaim, "It is finished," all Heaven would triumph. His ear caught the distant music and the shouts of victory in the heavenly courts. He knew that the knell of Satan's empire would then be sounded, and the name of Christ would be heralded from world to world throughout the universe.

Christ rejoiced that He could do more for His followers than they could ask or think. He spoke with assurance, knowing that an almighty decree had been given before the world was made. He knew that truth, armed with the omnipotence of the Holy Spirit, would conquer in the contest with evil; and that the bloodstained banner would wave triumphantly over His followers. He knew that the life of His trusting disciples would be like His, a series of uninterrupted victories, not seen to be such here, but recognized as such in the great hereafter...

Christ did not fail, neither was He discouraged, and His followers are to manifest a faith of the same enduring nature. They are to live as He lived, and work as He worked, because they depend on Him as the great Master Worker. Courage, energy, and perseverance they must possess. *Though apparent impossibilities obstruct their way, by His grace they are to go forward.* Instead of deploring difficulties, they are called upon to surmount them. They are to despair of nothing, and to hope for everything. With the golden chain of His matchless love Christ has bound them to the throne of God. It is His purpose that the highest influence in the universe, emanating from the Source of all power, shall be theirs. They are to have power to resist evil, power that neither Earth, nor death, nor Hell can master, power that will enable them to overcome as Christ overcame.[42]

III. SUCCESS THROUGH FAILURE

Promises in God's Word make it abundantly clear that God never fails those who are connected with Him. Our all-knowing, all-powerful, and all-loving God never fails and cannot fail because He is a God Who never sleeps nor slumbers. He knows every circumstance and situation of their lives. His

PROMISES IN GOD'S WORD
MAKE IT ABUNDANTLY CLEAR
THAT GOD NEVER FAILS THOSE WHO
ARE CONNECTED WITH HIM.

timing never fails, for His Providence makes His timing always perfect at any period of our lives. And His plans know no delay, for He is always on schedule, fulfilling His plan in the lives of His children. How can He fail? Here are a few of the passages:

"*He never fails.*" (ZEPHANIAH 3:5, NKJV)

"*I will never fail you nor forsake you.*" (HEBREWS 13:5, RSV)

"Be strong and of good courage, do not fear or be in dread of them: for it is the Lord your God Who goes with you; *He will not fail you or forsake you.*" (DEUTERONOMY 31:6, RSV)

"No man shall be able to stand before you all the days of your life; as I was with Moses, so I will be with you; *I will not fail you or forsake you.*" (JOSHUA 1:5, RSV)

These are not idle promises. God never fails. He never forsakes. He is there in good times and bad times. When we walk through the fire or in dangerous waters. In grief or sorrow, in difficulty or pain, in disappointment and death, He is there with us. With a God such as our God, how can we fail when we're connected with Him?

Below are some inspirational nuggets, showing that God knows no failure, apparent failure is a learning experience, we can succeed through failure, and that as long as *we remain connected with God* and cherish no attitude of self-pity, there can indeed be no failure with God.

1. GOD KNOWS NO FAILURE

We need not keep our own record of trials and difficulties, griefs, and sorrows. All these things are written in the books, and Heaven will take care of them... Let the world see that life with Him is *no failure.*[43]

When we give ourselves wholly to God and in our work follow His directions, He makes Himself responsible for its accomplishment. *He would not have us conjecture as to the success of our honest endeavors. Not once should we even think of failure. We are to cooperate with One Who knows no failure.*[44]

The omnipotent power of the Holy Spirit is the defense of every contrite soul. Not one that in penitence and faith has claimed His protection will Christ permit to pass under the enemy's power. The Saviour is by the side of His tempted and tried ones. *With Him there can be no such thing as failure, loss, impossibility, or defeat; we can do all things through Him Who strengthens us.* When temptations and trials come, do not wait to adjust all the difficulties, but look to Jesus, your helper.[45]

2. APPARENT FAILURE IS A LEARNING EXPERIENCE

Sometimes He [God] trains His workers by bringing to them disappointment and *apparent failure.* It is His purpose that they shall learn to master difficulties.

Often men are tempted to falter before the perplexities and obstacles that confront them. But if they will hold the beginning of their confidence steadfast unto the end, God will make the way clear. *Success will come to them as they struggle against difficulties.*[46]

While God has given us our work to do in bearing our testimony to the people by pen and voice, others must come to bear burdens in connection with the cause. They should not become discouraged, but should endeavor to *learn by every apparent failure how to make a success of the next effort. And if they connect with the Source of wisdom, they will surely succeed.*[47]

3. WE CAN SUCCEED THROUGH FAILURE

The worker who knows the meaning of union with Christ, has a constantly increasing desire and capacity to grasp the meaning of service for God. His knowledge enlarges; for to grow in grace means to have an increased ability to understand the Scriptures. Such a one is indeed a laborer together with God. He realizes that he is but an instrument, and that he must be passive in the Master's hands. Trials come to him; for unless thus tested, he would never know his lack of wisdom and experience. But if he seeks the Lord with humility and trust, every trial will work for his good. He may sometimes seem to fail, but his apparent failure may be God's way of bringing him true advancement, and may mean a better knowledge of himself and a firmer trust in Heaven. He may still make mistakes, but he learns not to repeat these mistakes. He becomes stronger to resist evil, and others reap benefit from his example.[48]

Whatever your work, dear brethren and sisters, do it for the Master, and do your best. Do not overlook present, golden opportunities and let your life prove a failure, while you sit idly dreaming of ease and success in a work for which God has not fitted you. Do the work that is nearest. Do it, even though it may be amid the perils and hardships of the missionary field… Christ laid aside His glory, and came to this earth to suffer for sinners. If we meet with hardships in our work, let us look to Him Who is the Author and Finisher of our faith. Then *we shall not fail nor be discouraged.*[49]

If we have His care and His approval, we shall make a success wherever we are and in whatever we may engage. Without the blessing of God, any amount of prosperity will fail to be a success.[50]

4. DISCONNECTION WITH GOD THE CAUSE OF FAILURE

When I was down with my failure, one of my former students e-mailed me: "Failure is what a man sees. God sees our failure as a stepping-stone and uses it as a foundation for a greater success." This counsel from this student ties in well with the statement:

There is *no failure* with God.[51]

The above statement is unequivocal. It allows for no doubt or misinterpretation: "There is no failure with God." Period. But what does it mean? Does it mean that a believer in God, a spiritual person, or a Christian—a person who is "with God" or has a relationship with Him—can never or will never fail?

Not at all. It doesn't mean that a believer in God will not fail. Rather it means that as long as we *remain connected with* God there can be no real failure. For what appears to be a failure becomes a key, a stepping-stone essential to success. To paraphrase the words of Christ, as long as we abide in Him, as the branch to the Vine, we shall bear the fruits of success.

> Abide in Me, and I in you. As the branch cannot bear fruit of itself, unless it abides in the Vine, neither can you, unless you abide in Me. I am the Vine, you are the branches. He who abides in Me, and I in him, bears much fruit; for without Me you can do nothing. If anyone does not abide in Me, he is cast out as a branch and is withered; and they gather them and throw them into the fire, and they are burned.
> (JOHN 15:4–6)

Fruitlessness is failure or a lack of success. And it is the result of not abiding in Christ, that is, not maintaining connection with God. Or as we pointed out earlier, "Human strength is weakness, human wisdom is folly. Our success does not depend on our talents or learning, but on our living connection with God."[52]

Let's explain the same thing slightly differently. Using the analogy of spiritual failure (or sin) as representative of all other kinds of failures (academic, professional, marriage, etc.), the statement "There is no failure with God" simply means that we cannot fail (or sin) as long as we abide in Him or remain connected with Him.

> Whoever abides in Him does not sin… Whoever has been born of God does not sin, for His seed remains in him; and he cannot sin, because he has been born of God. (1 JOHN 3:6, 9)

The key is *abiding in Him*. Failure or sin results when we break our connection with Him through a lack of trust or faith. This is why "Every failure on the part of the children of God is due to their lack of faith."[53]

The whole purpose of Christian growth is to bring us to the point whereby we can have an implicit or unshakable faith in God, no matter what. This is a process or journey that never ends. Hence it is often referred to as a "walk" or "growth in grace" (what theologians refer to as sanctification or Christian perfection).[54]

> FAILURE OCCURS THE MOMENT WE CEASE
> TO IMPROVE UPON OUR BEST EFFORT.
> FAILURE IS SETTLING FOR GOOD WHEN BETTER
> IS AVAILABLE. FAILURE IS THE MINDSET THAT
> ALLOWS NO ROOM FOR IMPROVEMENT.

The Bible uses the imagery of a "walk" to *emphasize motion*.[55] The Christian life is a *movement* towards a particular goal. It is a journey towards a particular destination. That destination or goal is to be Christlike. It means reflecting Christ's life of love and humility, courage and self-control, and His compassion and purity.

It is this life that is called the victorious Christian life. True success, then, for the Christian, is to reflect the character of Christ in every aspect of life.

The key to this Christian walk, this abiding in Christ, is to bring us to the point where there can actually be "no possibility of failure" (or sin) in our lives.[56] This is possible through a daily, or constant, dependence on God.

Thus, when we say, "There is *no failure* with God," we simply mean that when we depend on ourselves, there can be no success. We can do nothing. Only failure will result. But when we depend on Him we will not fail, for failures (or setbacks) will be merely *apparent ones*.

Knowing that with God there is no real failure can be a very strong motivation for us not to give up. It inspires us to muster strength and move beyond our seeming failures. It provides us with a determination to persevere. It allows us to convert setbacks into stepping-stones that lead to success.

⌐ 5. LACK OF IMPROVEMENT THE MINDSET OF FAILURE

If success is a constant growth, then lack of growth is failure. Contentedness or satisfaction with where we are in our spiritual lives or what we have accomplished in our professional careers is evidence of failure. Failure occurs the moment we cease to improve upon our best effort. Failure is settling for good when better is available. *Failure is the mindset that allows no room for improvement.*

Again, we can use the analogy of a Christian's growth or walk (or Christian sanctification) to explain the meaning of failure as a lack of growth.

Rooted in Christ, we must grow like the small seed that germinates from the soil. When it begins to grow, there is first the blade, then the ear, after that the full corn in the ear. As long as the plant is responding to all the resources available for its development, it is considered perfect at each stage of its growth. Thus it is with the Christian life. E. G. White explains:

> We cannot expect instantaneous sanctification, but we must grow like the grain, as represented by Christ—first the blade, then the ear, then the full grain—and thus perfect a Christian character. We must become intelligent and earnest to know what our duty is and then walk in obedience to God's holy will.[57]

> *The growth of Christian character is gradual—like the advancement of the natural plant through its various stages of development. But nevertheless the progress is continual. As in nature, so it is in grace, the plant must either grow or die.*

> Day by day the sanctifying influence of the Spirit of God almost imperceptibly leads those who love the ways of truth toward the perfection of righteousness, till finally the soul is ripe for the harvest, the lifework is ended, God gathers in His grain. *There is no period in the Christian life when there is no more to learn, no higher attainments to reach. Sanctification is the work of a lifetime.* First the blade, then the ear, then

the full corn in the ear, then the ripening and the harvest; for when the fruit is perfect, it is ready for the sickle.[58]

Paraphrasing the last point and using the language of success and failure, *There is no period in the Christian life when there is no more to learn, no higher attainments to reach.* True success or excellence is the work of a lifetime. Conversely, a lack of growth, the ceasing to improve one's lot, is failure.

And so, Biblically speaking, true success does not mean that persons have arrived at a stage in their lives where they cannot grow any further or improve upon their endeavors. *Failure is guaranteed by a self-satisfied mindset that allows no room for improvement.* For failure thinks there is no room for further progress.

6. SELF-PITY, THE ATTITUDE TO FAILURE

Many greatly magnify seeming difficulties and then begin to pity themselves and give way to despondency. Such need to make an entire change in themselves. They need to discipline themselves to put forth exertion and to overcome all childish feelings. They should determine that life shall not be spent in working at trifles....

Everyone should have an aim, an object, in life. The loins of the mind should be girded up and the thoughts be trained to keep to the point, as the compass to the pole. The mind should be directed in the right channel, according to well-formed plans. Then every step will be a step in advance...

Success or failure in this life depends much upon the manner in which the thoughts are disciplined.[59]

Success in any line demands a definite aim. *People who achieve true success in life keep steadily in view the aim worthy of their endeavor.* Such an aim is set before the young people of today. The Heaven-appointed purpose of giving the Gospel to the world in this generation is the noblest that can appeal to any human being. It opens a field of effort to everyone whose heart Christ has touched.[60]

God's purpose for the children growing up in our homes is wider, deeper, higher, than our restricted vision has comprehended. From the humblest lot those whom He has seen faithful have in times past been called to witness for Him in the world's highest places. And many a young person of today, growing up as did Daniel in his Judean home, studying God's Word and His works, and learning the lessons of faithful service, will stand in legislative assemblies, in halls of justice, or in royal courts, as a witness for the King of kings. Multitudes will be called to a wider ministry. The whole world is opening to the Gospel.[61]

In the darkest days, when appearances seem most forbidding, *have faith in God. He is working out His will, doing all things well in behalf of His people.* The strength of those who love and serve Him will be renewed day by day.[62]

He is able and willing to bestow upon His servants all the help they need. He will give them the wisdom which their varied necessities demand.[63]

Christ's method alone will give true success in reaching the people. The Saviour mingled with men as one who desired their good. He showed His sympathy for them, ministered to their needs, and won their confidence. Then He bade them, "Follow Me."[64]

LEARNING FROM FAILURE OR LEARNING FROM SUCCESS?

At the beginning of this chapter, we mentioned that history affords many sources that address questions about success and failure. However, the verdict from these sources, while at times compelling, can also be confusing, if not contradictory. Because of human limitations, we cannot always trust human sources to provide reliable answers. For the Christian, therefore, it is safe to assert that all conclusions must be evaluated by the truth of Scripture.

As we conclude the discussion in this chapter of *Six More Chances*, let me illustrate the Christian approach by using contemporary research to attempt the answer to one important question: Should we learn from failure or learn from success? The answers proffered by this research will be carefully weighed against the teachings of Scripture.

Verdict From Contemporary Research

Researchers are unanimous that we should learn from both success and failure, although when it comes to *changing human behavior*, the evidence seems to suggest that much more can be learned from success. For example, after reviewing investigations by different researchers, Stephen J. Gill, a consultant on human performance improvement, states the following:

> We learn more from studying successes than we do from studying failure… However, a case can be made for both… The focus on failure might be necessary when reviewing disasters and developing products. However, when evaluating behavior change in individuals, teams, and organizations, usually much more can be gained from a focus on success. People can explain why they changed their behavior much more readily than why they didn't change. And they're much more willing to talk and much more honest about successes than failures given the human propensity to negatively judge people who are not successful.[65]

Notice that the above researcher is not discounting learning lessons from failure. We must learn from both success and failure. What he is simply emphasizing is that, when it comes to *human behavior*, much more can be learned from the successes of others than from their failures.

MIT researcher J. Nathan Matias further confirms the above view. In the concluding thoughts of his rhetorical article, "Why Learn from Failure, When You Can Learn from Success?" he acknowledges that the title of his article is "a bit of a false dilemma for the sake of argument. In reality, we all learn from a complex mix of success and failure alike… It's impossible to learn from just success or just failure… Reflection on both success and failure is a winning combination."[66]

Like the previous researcher, Matias also mentions that, though we learn from both success and failure, if one has to choose the better source, success has the upper hand.

Furthermore, in an apparent rebuttal to the oft-quoted statement popularized by a 2007 Walt Disney movie, *Meet the Robinsons*—"*From failing you* learn. From success, not so much"—Matias responds that "failure is a poor teacher" and "learning from failure is overrated in the startup world, and that success is the best teacher of all."

These two ideas about whether or not we are most benefited by learning from success (Gill and Matias) or from failure (*Meet the Robinsons*) may seem contradictory. However, when we observe that the two ideas stem from different emphases, the problem doesn't look as confusing.

The apparent contradiction is resolved when we realize what is going on in the *Meet the Robinsons* movie from which the quote comes. The main character, little Lewis, is a twelve-year-old orphan. He spends the majority of his time inventing things that almost always turn out to be failures. His eventual discovery comes when he is given the advice: "From failing, you learn. From success, not so much."

Put differently, when it comes to things, products, inventions, etc.,

It is a mistake to suppose that men succeed through success; they much oftener succeed through failures. Precept, study, advice, and example could never have taught them so well as failure has done.
—*Samuel Smiles*

Every failure affords an opportunity to learn and grow. Failure keeps us humble. It enables us to see the world—and ourselves—more clearly. In the words of Paul Schoemaker, author of the book Brilliant *Mistakes: Finding Success on the Far Side of Failure,*

The school of hard knocks is a great teacher, even if the tuition is very high, precisely because the lessons make such a deep imprint. We need emotion born of direct, difficult experience to internalize, remember, and learn.

In other words, the argument that we learn more *from failure* than success seems more applicable to products and inventions, than to human behavior—which seems to be the focus of Matias and Gill. In fact, Matias indicates, among other things, that his emphasis is more on people and teams—to encourage apprenticeships, mentorship, and perhaps experienced consultants. In this respect, he states:

Earned success is a much better teacher. It offers nuanced insight and the experienced growth of capabilities rather than broad brushstrokes on what to avoid. Failure might teach us to hire a good tech team. Success can teach us how to hire a good tech team. Failure might teach us to avoid bad community relations. Success can teach us helpful forms of good community relations which we should seek out.[67]

> THE SAFEST COURSE, THROUGH THE AGES, HAS BEEN TO EMBRACE CONCLUSIONS FROM HUMAN SOURCES, IF AND ONLY IF, THEY ARE IN HARMONY WITH THE WORD OF GOD.

Although Matias argues for learning more *from success* than from failure, he recognizes the limitations of learning from success. In the same article he writes: "To be fair, success can also [sic] blind, and lucky success is the hardest to replicate." As a Christian, what this suggests to me is that even when learning from success we must be careful.

To sum up, we've been looking at how contemporary research addresses the question: Should we learn from failure or learn from success? We've seen that care is needed in how we evaluate the answers provided to this particular question. Otherwise we come away confused. In some cases, such seemingly contradictory verdicts can be fatal.

The Christian's approach is to appeal to a better teacher or source on issues of success and failure. It is instructive to look at the Scriptures because they are the most dependable source of authority, and not just because they are merely another source of reference. The safest course, through the ages, has been to embrace conclusions from human sources, if and only if, they are in harmony with the Word of God. For the former have often failed; only the latter endures forever.

Verdict From Holy Scripture

The Bible argues similarly that we must learn from both the failures and mistakes of its characters, as well as from their successes. It, however, cautions us in how we learn from successes. Since even the best of human beings experience failure—the spiritual failure of sin—no human being can be a perfect model of success. The only Model of true success is our Lord Jesus Christ. We must always learn from Him because He alone never once failed.

Learning From Failures

The Word of God, the Christian's only dependable source of authority, invites us to learn from the failures of people who lived in Old Testament times, as the apostle Paul wrote:

> Now all these things happened to them as examples, and they were written for our admonition [warning, caution, reprimand, rebuke, reproach, scolding], upon whom the ends of the ages have come. Therefore let him who thinks he stands *take heed* lest he fall. (1 CORINTHIANS 10:11, 12, NKJV)

Notice that the above passage begins with the words, "Now all these things happened to them…" and bids us to "take heed" (i.e., learn). The "them" in this particular passage refers to all those who lived in Old Testament times. But it also includes those who lived in the days of the New Testament, the record of whose lives and actions are preserved in Holy Scripture. Space limitations prevent me from listing "them." But we can recognize "them" by things that happened to them when they did "all these things."

What are the "all these things" that happened to them, and about which we are to "take heed"? When we start from verse 1 of First Corinthians chapter ten, we discover the kinds of things we are being warned against:

- LUST [V. 6]
- IDOLATRY [V. 7]
- SEXUAL IMMORALITY [V. 8]
- PROVOCATION OF GOD, AS IN GRUMBLING AND UNGRATEFULNESS [V. 9; cf. Numbers 21]
- UNNECESSARY COMPLAINTS AND UNBELIEF [V. 10]

These are by no means the only sins of which we are warned to "take heed." The Bible lists other human behaviors we should avoid—the failures that are amplified in the lives of some Bible characters. They are failures for which God "gave them up":

> God abandoned them to their shameful desires. Even the women turned against the natural way to have sex and instead indulged in sex with each other. And the men, instead of having normal sexual relations with women, burned with lust for each other. Men did shameful things with other men, and as a result of this sin, they suffered within themselves the penalty they deserved.
>
> Since they thought it foolish to acknowledge God, He abandoned them to their foolish thinking and let them do things that should never be done. Their lives became full of every kind of wickedness, sin, greed, hate, envy, murder, quarreling, deception, malicious behavior, and gossip. They are backstabbers, haters of God, insolent, proud, and boastful. They invent new ways of sinning, and they disobey their parents. They refuse to understand, break their promises, are heartless, and have no mercy. They know God's justice requires that those who do these things deserve to die, yet they do them anyway. Worse yet, they encourage others to do them, too. (ROMANS 1:26–32)

The New Testament Scriptures indicate that the things happening to "them" who did these things in Old Testament times are for our instruction. *We are to learn from their failures.* "For whatever things were written before were written *for our learning,* that we through the patience and comfort of the Scriptures might have hope" (ROMANS 15:4).

> But know this, that in the last days perilous times will come: For men will be lovers of themselves, lovers of money, boasters, proud, blasphemers, disobedient to parents, unthankful, unholy, unloving, unforgiving, slanderers, without self-control, brutal, despisers of good, traitors, headstrong, haughty, lovers of pleasure rather than lovers of God, having a form of godliness but denying its power. And from such people turn away! (2 TIMOTHY 3:1–5)

When you follow the desires of your sinful nature, the results are very clear: sexual immorality, impurity, lustful pleasures, idolatry, sorcery, hostility, quarreling, jealousy, outbursts of anger, selfish ambition, dissension, division, envy, drunkenness, wild parties, and other sins like these. Let me tell you again, as I have before, that anyone living that sort of life will not inherit the Kingdom of God. (GALATIANS 5:19-21; 2 TIMOTHY 3:1-7)

The Bible offers these warnings for our instruction, that is: "Now all these things happened to them as examples, and they were written for our admonition, upon whom the ends of the ages have come. Therefore let him who thinks he stands take heed lest he fall" (1 CORINTHIANS 10:11, 12).

Whenever we see "therefore" in Scripture, we must ask what it is "there for." In the above passage, the word "therefore" suggests a conclusion. When the apostle Paul says, "Therefore let him who thinks he stands take heed lest he fall," he simply means that Scripture was written so that we might learn from *failures*—the failures of the Bible characters—and be warned by their mistakes.

Learning From Successes

The Bible also invites us to learn from the successes or triumphs of its heroes and heroines. One place this is clearly asserted is Hebrews 11. This chapter on faith can also be seen as a chapter on triumph, victory, or success. The chapter is an invitation to *learn from those who did things right*.

We must go to Scripture and study about how these Bible heroes and heroines succeeded. How they triumphed over failures. The entire chapter of Hebrews 11 reads:

> Faith is the confidence that what we hope for will actually happen; it gives us assurance about things we cannot see. Through their faith, the people in days of old earned a good reputation.
>
> By faith we understand that the entire universe was formed at God's command, that what we now see did not come from anything that can be seen.
>
> It was by faith that Abel brought a more acceptable offering to God than Cain did. Abel's offering gave evidence that he was a righteous

man, and God showed His approval of his gifts. Although Abel is long dead, he still speaks to us by his example of faith.

It was by faith that Enoch was taken up to Heaven without dying— "he disappeared, because God took him." For before he was taken up, he was known as a person who pleased God. And it is impossible to please God without faith. Anyone who wants to come to Him must believe that God exists and that He rewards those who sincerely seek Him.

It was by faith that Noah built a large boat to save his family from the Flood. He obeyed God, Who warned him about things that had never happened before. By his faith Noah condemned the rest of the world, and he received the righteousness that comes by faith.

> HEBREWS 11 IS A CHAPTER ON FAITH.
> IT CAN ALSO BE SEEN AS A CHAPTER ON
> TRIUMPH, VICTORY, OR SUCCESS.
> THE CHAPTER IS AN INVITATION TO LEARN
> FROM THOSE WHO DID THINGS RIGHT.

It was by faith that Abraham obeyed when God called him to leave home and go to another land that God would give him as his inheritance. He went without knowing where he was going. And even when he reached the land God promised him, he lived there by faith—for he was like a foreigner, living in tents. And so did Isaac and Jacob, who inherited the same promise. Abraham was confidently looking forward to a city with eternal foundations, a city designed and built by God.

It was by faith that even Sarah was able to have a child, though she was barren and was too old. She believed that God would keep His promise. And so a whole nation came from this one man who was as good as dead—a nation with so many people that, like the stars in the sky and the sand on the seashore, there is no way to count them.

All these people died still believing what God had promised them. They did not receive what was promised, but they saw it all from a distance and welcomed it. They agreed that they were foreigners and nomads here on Earth. Obviously people who say such things are looking forward to a country they can call their own. If they had longed for the country they came from, they could have gone back. But they were looking for a better place, a heavenly homeland. That is why God is not ashamed to be called their God, for He has prepared a city for them.

> THE HEROES AND HEROINES OF FAITH IN HEBREWS 11 WERE CHAMPIONS IN ACCOMPLISHMENTS. WINNERS IN GRUELING COMPETITIONS. VICTORS IN THE SPIRITUAL RACE. "ALL THESE PEOPLE EARNED A GOOD REPUTATION BECAUSE OF THEIR FAITH" (V. 39).

It was by faith that Abraham offered Isaac as a sacrifice when God was testing him. Abraham, who had received God's promises, was ready to sacrifice his only son, Isaac, even though God had told him, "Isaac is the son through whom your descendants will be counted." Abraham reasoned that if Isaac died, God was able to bring him back to life again And in a sense, Abraham did receive his son back from the dead.

It was by faith that Isaac promised blessings for the future to his sons, Jacob and Esau.

It was by faith that Jacob, when he was old and dying, blessed each of Joseph's sons and bowed in worship as he leaned on his staff.

It was by faith that Joseph, when he was about to die, said confidently that the people of Israel would leave Egypt. He even commanded them to take his bones with them when they left.

It was by faith that Moses' parents hid him for three months when he was born. They saw that God had given them an unusual child, and they were not afraid to disobey the king's command.

It was by faith that Moses, when he grew up, refused to be called the son of Pharaoh's daughter. He chose to share the oppression of God's people instead of enjoying the fleeting pleasures of sin. He thought it was better to suffer for the sake of Christ than to own the treasures of Egypt, for he was looking ahead to his great reward. It was by faith that Moses left the land of Egypt, not fearing the king's anger. He kept right on going because he kept his eyes on the One Who is invisible. It was by faith that Moses commanded the people of Israel to keep the Passover and to sprinkle blood on the doorposts so that the angel of death would not kill their firstborn sons.

It was by faith that the people of Israel went right through the Red Sea as though they were on dry ground. But when the Egyptians tried to follow, they were all drowned.

It was by faith that the people of Israel marched around Jericho for seven days, and the walls came crashing down.

It was by faith that Rahab the prostitute was not destroyed with the people in her city who refused to obey God. For she had given a friendly welcome to the spies.

How much more do I need to say? It would take too long to recount the stories of the faith of Gideon, Barak, Samson, Jephthah, David, Samuel, and all the prophets. By faith these people overthrew kingdoms, ruled with justice, and received what God had promised them. They shut the mouths of lions, quenched the flames of fire, and escaped death by the edge of the sword. Their weakness was turned to strength. They became strong in battle and put whole armies to flight. Women received their loved ones back again from death.

But others were tortured, refusing to turn from God in order to be set free. They placed their hope in a better life after the resurrection. Some were jeered at, and their backs were cut open with whips. Others were chained in prisons. Some died by stoning, some were sawed in half, and others were killed with the sword. Some went about wearing skins of sheep and goats, destitute and oppressed and mistreated. They were too good for this world, wandering over deserts and mountains, hiding in caves and holes in the ground.

All these people earned a good reputation because of their faith, yet none of them received all that God had promised. For God had something better in mind for us, so that they would not reach perfection without us.

If there's one sentence to summarize this Hebrews 11 chapter, it is this: *Learn from their successes.* They were heroes and heroines of faith. Champions in accomplishments. Winners in grueling competitions. Victors in the spiritual race. "All these people earned a good reputation because of their faith" (v. 39).

Caution in Learning From Successes

In Scripture, there's a place to learn from failures, and another from successes. These are not mutually exclusive.

Notice, however, that, even though all the Bible characters mentioned in Hebrews 11 excelled in faith (and, by the way, the list is by no means exhaustive, as verse 32 tells us), even though we can learn from their successes, just as contemporary researchers have cautioned, we must be careful when we study the successes or triumphs of these Bible characters.

As I will show in another book, even the best of God's people failed. From Adam's day to the last Bible character mentioned in Scripture, every human being experienced failures in their lives. To name some: Eve, Noah, Abraham, Moses, David, Solomon, Elijah, Hezekiah, John the Baptist, Peter, Martha, Paul, and more. "For everyone has sinned; we all fall short of God's glorious standard" (ROMANS 3:23). As the Scriptures say,

No one is righteous—
not even one.
No one is truly wise;
no one is seeking God.
All have turned away;
all have become useless.
No one does good,
not a single one.
Their talk is foul, like the stench from an open grave.
Their tongues are filled with lies.

Snake venom drips from their lips.
Their mouths are full of cursing and bitterness.
They rush to commit murder.
Destruction and misery always follow them.
They don't know where to find peace.
They have no fear of God at all.
(ROMANS 3:10–18)

Because "all have sinned," because all have deviated from God's standard of success, because there is not a single individual since the Fall of Adam who never failed (the Bible says, "No one is righteous—not even one"), not even the best of the human race can be a perfect model of success. But there's one exception.

The only One Who can be an Example of true or perfect success is Jesus Christ. He alone never once failed. He is our only true Model of success: *"Looking unto Jesus* the Author and Finisher of our faith; Who for the joy that was set before Him endured the cross, despising the shame, and is set down at the right hand of the throne of God. For *consider* Him that endured such contradiction of sinners against Himself, lest ye be wearied and faint in your minds" (HEBREWS 12:2, 3).

> THE ONLY ONE WHO CAN BE AN EXAMPLE
> OF TRUE OR PERFECT SUCCESS IS JESUS CHRIST.
> HE ALONE NEVER ONCE FAILED.

JESUS CHRIST, THE MODEL OF TRUE SUCCESS

Failure is deviation from expected and desired results, and may be viewed as the opposite of success. Sacred Scripture makes it abundantly clear that all have sinned—that is, *all* have failed. All have come short of the glory of God. Since failure is deviation from expected and desired results, the only One Who can be the Model to learn about success (victory over sin or failure) is Jesus Christ.

> For God called you to do good, even if it means suffering, just as Christ suffered for you. He is your Example, and you must follow in His steps.
> He never sinned,
> nor ever deceived anyone.
> He did not retaliate when He was insulted,
> nor threaten revenge when He suffered.
> He left His case in the hands of God,
> Who always judges fairly.
> He personally carried our sins
> in His body on the cross
> so that we can be dead to sin
> and live for what is right.
> By His wounds
> you are healed.
> Once you were like sheep
> who wandered away.
> But now you have turned to your Shepherd,
> the Guardian of your souls.
> (1 PETER 2:21–25, NLT)

Notice again what the Bible says about Christ: "He is your Example, and you must follow in His steps. He never sinned, nor ever deceived anyone …" (vv. 21, 22). He never once sinned; He never once experienced failure. This is why He is our Model of true success.

In the book *Steps to Christ*, a life-changing masterpiece on successful Christian living—Ellen G. White writes concerning Christ:

> "Love, mercy, and compassion were revealed in every act of His life. His heart went out in tender sympathy to the children of men. He took man's nature, that He might reach man's wants. The poorest and humblest were not afraid to approach Him. Even little children were attracted to Him. They loved to climb upon His knees and gaze into the pensive face, benignant with love."[68]

The book continues:

> He exercised the greatest tact and thoughtful, kind attention in His intercourse with the people.
>
> He was never rude, never needlessly spoke a severe word, never gave needless pain to a sensitive soul. He did not censure human weakness.
>
> He spoke the truth, but always in love.
>
> He denounced hypocrisy, unbelief, and iniquity; but tears were in His voice as He uttered His scathing rebukes.
>
> He wept over Jerusalem, the city He loved, which refused to receive Him, the Way, the Truth, and the Life. They had rejected Him, the Saviour, but He regarded them with pitying tenderness.
>
> His life was one of self-denial and thoughtful care for others. Every soul was precious in His eyes. While He ever bore Himself with divine dignity, He bowed with the tenderest regard to every member of the family of God. In all men He saw fallen souls whom it was His mission to save. (*STEPS TO CHRIST*, P. 12.1)[69]

Christ manifested true love in His life of total selflessness. He gave selflessly of His time, His energy, and His life. He was humble, kind, patient, and never rude. Truly, His life is a perfect model of what God views as success.

One of the most beautiful pictures ever painted about Christ's matchless character is found in the following words of Ellen G. White. Notice how harmoniously Christ combined in His life apparently conflicting qualities.

> Jesus was a perfect pattern of what we should be,
> He was the strictest observer of His Father's law,
> yet He moved in perfect freedom.
> He had all the fervor of the enthusiast,
> yet He was calm, sober, and self-possessed.
> He was elevated above the common affairs of the world,
> yet He did not exclude Himself from society.
> He dined with publicans and sinners,
> played with little children, and took them in His arms and blessed them.
> He graced the wedding feast with His presence.

He shed tears at the grave of Lazarus.

He was a lover of the beautiful in nature and used the lilies
to illustrate the value of natural simplicity in the sight of God, above
artificial display.

He used the occupation of the husbandman
to illustrate the most sublime truths…

His zeal never degenerated into passion
nor His consistency into selfish obstinacy.

His benevolence never savored of weakness
nor His sympathy of sentimentalism.

He combined the innocence and simplicity of the child
with manly strength,

[He combined His] all-absorbing devotion to God
with tender love for man.

He possessed commanding dignity combined
with winning grace of humility.

He manifested unyielding firmness
with gentleness.

May we live daily in close connection with this perfect,
faultless character.

We have not six patterns to follow, nor five;
we have only one, and that is Christ Jesus.
(E. G. WHITE, *IN HEAVENLY PLACES*, P. 54.3–5)[70]

Therefore, if we want to understand the nature of true success, we must look at the beautiful life of our Lord Jesus Christ. This is why, connected with Him, we can never fail.

.

CHAPTER 3

∾

BEYOND ULTIMATE FAILURE

Where Is Your Hope?

(The Decisive Question on the Issues of Life and Death)

A PAIN FAR WORSE THAN DEATH

When I experienced my personal failure and resigned from my work as the director of a ministry to public university students, the pain I experienced could only be compared to death. I described my experience of failure as a "pain far worse than death." For death is the most dreadful reality we know. Perhaps the best way to capture the pain of my spiritual failure is to quote excerpts from my public announcement:

It is with deep pain—a pain far worse than death—that I have to resign at this critical time. Many of our standard bearers are being laid to rest, others are retiring and growing old, thousands of young people are calling for spiritual mentorship from faithful and courageous adult leaders, doors that are now opened for God's work will soon be forever shut, and the cause of God urgently needs more faithful laborers in the field and within the church. Now shouldn't be the time to resign. But I believe my decision is in the best interest of God's work, and is consistent with the Biblical teachings and messages I have shared by voice and by pen.

Undoubtedly, my resignation will be greeted with deep sorrow and hurt by those of you who have known me and worked closely with me. On the other hand, others who have always opposed what we stand for will have an additional reason to rejoice. For this, I am deeply sorry. Pray that the Lord will grant me genuine sorrow and humility of heart as I wait patiently on Him. Pray also that God's faithful people everywhere—especially the young people whose lives I've touched—will learn important lessons from my experience, be comforted and encouraged by the Lord Himself, and be strengthened to carry forward the work of a "Bible-based revival movement in which every student is a missionary." Pray that the treasures of truth that have been faithfully delivered would not be rejected nor ignored on account of the damaged vessel that carried them, and that the Lord will renew my strength, restoring me again to full health—physically and spiritually.

> TO MOST PEOPLE, DEATH IS THE ULTIMATE FAILURE—THE FAILURE OF DREAMS, HOPES, HEALTH, AND LIFE ITSELF. BUT IS IT?

To most people, death is the ultimate failure—the failure of dreams, hopes, health, and life itself. And the consequences of failure—especially mega-failures—can inflict "pain far worse than death."

The emotions behind my spiritual failure are mainly from my brushes with the death and threat of death of loved ones. Most importantly is that of the profound experience related above. It almost defies description; the experience was very gripping. It was a pain almost unimaginable in its intensity and unbelievable in its reality. I wished for death.

The dread of death is foremost in the list of fears that confront humanity. Beyond any form of loss, we do not want death to knock on our doors or that of our loved ones. It has come to be known as the ultimate failure, since it represents total cessation and, often, irreplaceable loss. Money cannot stop it from claiming its victim, prestige cannot bargain with it, and age cannot defy it.

Death has claimed the best of men and the worst of the lot. The rich and poor have felt its sting; prince and pauper feel its imminence with their every breath. Of all the failures in the life of man, death bears the unequaled stamp as the ultimate failure.

But is death really the end? Is death the worst thing that could happen to anyone? Is there hope beyond ultimate failure? If so, where can we find such a hope?

This chapter ponders the question "Where is your hope?" When all else fails and physical death comes or you suffer losses that inflict pain far worse than death, where is your hope? The question is not *what* is your hope, but *where* is your hope? That is, do you have a *foundation* for your hope? Do you know *why* you have this hope?

DO YOU KNOW WHY?

The content of this chapter draws largely from a Bible lecture I have given on public university campuses and other locations around the world. It ponders the question *"Do You Know WHY?"* I emphasize the word "Why" because it is one of the most important questions for everyone living in this world.

The adverb "Why" is used as an interrogative particle to probe the reason behind an action or idea. It seeks to find the purpose or cause of something. Everyone asks "why" questions:

~ When children ask "why," it can be a sign of their inquisitiveness.

~ When teenagers or young adults ask their parents "why," it can either be a sign of rebellion or a search for their own identity.

~ When adults ask "why," it is often a sign of powerlessness or frustration.

Regardless of who is asking "why," that question implies a search for answers. The importance of finding answers to "why" questions is best stated in the following three quotes:

"He who has a *WHY* to live can bear almost any *HOW*."
—*Friedrich Nietzsche*

"He who knows HOW will always have a job; but he who knows WHY will always be the boss."
—SKP

"There are two great days in a person's life—the day we are born and the day we discover *WHY.*"
—*William Barclay*

The first time I seriously raised some "Why" questions was in 2006, when I presented five Bible lectures to a group of students at Harvard University. Here are the questions I asked:

1. WHY DWELL ON A WRITTEN PAST, WHEN YOU CAN WRITE THE FUTURE?
2. WHY SETTLE FOR GOOD, WHEN BETTER IS AVAILABLE?
3. WHY CONTINUE ON THE WRONG WAY, WHEN A U-TURN IS POSSIBLE?
4. WHY KEEP SILENT, WHEN MILLIONS RISK DEATH?
5. WHY MAKE A DUMB DECISION, WHEN YOU'RE SO SMART?

Since then, I have directed many more "Why" questions to different audiences around the world. Thus, in the context of our discussion of death as ultimate failure, it is important to raise the decisive question of WHY anyone can believe there is hope beyond such failures.

I've given this rather long introduction to make the point that understanding the reason behind something is very important. We simply cannot ignore answering the question "why?"

Not surprisingly, the Bible also contains many "whys." For example,

God asked Cain: "Why is your countenance sad?"

- Ezekiel: "Why will you die?"

- Jesus: "My God, My God, why?…"

- Angel at the tomb: "Why seek ye the living among the dead?"

- Resurrected Christ: "Saul, Saul, why are you persecuting Me?"

So back to the WHY question inherent in our very first question: "Where is your hope?" Do you have a *foundation* for your hope? Do you know *why* you have this hope? "Do you know WHY?" If not, now is the time.

WAKE-UP CALLS

At least once in a lifetime, certain earthshaking tragedies occur in the experiences of every individual, family, business, church, and nation. These tragedies or disasters are so disturbing that they arrest our attention in a compelling way. Usually, life ceases to be business as usual after such events. These earth-shattering experiences are known as *wake-up calls*. Wake-up calls challenge the status quo and redefine how the individual or group conducts itself from a given point onward.

One such event occurred on the morning of September 11, 2001. In a single hour the United States, and indeed the whole world, were forever changed by carefully executed terrorist attacks on the World Trade Center in New York and the Pentagon in Washington, D.C. September 11 was a wake-up call.

In the moments after the terrorist attack …

- people stayed away from movie theaters; they didn't want to see movies;

- major sporting events were also cancelled; apparently, many sports fans suddenly realized that some things are more important than football, baseball, or basketball;

- married couples who had earlier filed for divorces withdrew their divorce cases from the courts and started working on reconciliation;

~ people who were not known to show interest in religious things suddenly were searching for God; for some strange reasons the philosophies of atheism, agnosticism, secular humanism, etc., became untenable;

~ church attendance shot up; the only place people wanted to go was to church; some churches had to conduct multiple services;

~ nobody had to resort to some ridiculous, so-called "innovative" gospel gimmicks to attract young people to church; there was no need for such gospel gimmicks as gospel clowns, gospel magicians, gospel comedies, etc. Even the most ardent enthusiasts of contemporary rock music in the church suddenly realized that old-fashioned hymn singing was not old-fashioned after all!

~ in our own church, members who never cared about Bible prophecies and end-time events suddenly started studying the books of Daniel and Revelation, and E. G. White's insightful book *The Great Controversy*.

Businesses also hear their own wake-up calls. Sometimes, all it takes is a major investments loss, or the arrival of an aggressive business competitor. Suddenly, nothing is business as usual anymore.

Families receive wake-up calls when the tranquility and joy of the home is suddenly shattered by the shocking news of adultery, betrayal, divorce, or death. When things like this happen, life ceases to be normal for children as well as parents.

Individuals also experience certain tragedies that serve as wake up calls:

~ accidents; devastation from disasters (wars, earthquakes, hurricanes, fires, etc.)

~ sudden illness; when the doctor tells you, "I'm sorry but the test results suggest that you have cancer," or "You have contracted HIV/AIDS"

~ failure in important exams (e.g., MCAT, LSAT, GCE, O-Levels, etc.) shattering the hopes of students; or failure on job interviews

- politicians experience shocking defeat at the hands of some un-known underdogs

- etc.

MY PERSONAL WAKE-UP CALL

There are also *personal* wake-up calls—tragedies that hit close to home. Not too long ago, I received my own devastating wake-up call. To date, I have only shared it with a few people. It happened when my wife went for her annual physical checkup. Everything seemed normal, until the doctor wanted to speak with both of us. Then he announced, "I'm sorry, but it appears that Rebecca has cancer, and it appears that it is far advanced."

Even though the doctor tried to assure us that some patients have survived such cancers, and even though he proceeded to outline some options of treatment for our consideration, I cannot recall anything else he said after he had announced that Becky had what seemed like *terminal cancer*. We were very silent as we drove home.

In the days after the diagnosis, my wife's attitude and behavior changed remarkably.

The clothes in her closet lost their appeal. She realized that a terminally ill cancer patient needs more than clothes. Her eating habits changed; she became more particular about health and lifestyle concerns.

She also started calling up individuals who have hurt her and reconciling with them. Her prayer life also changed. Though she has always been a woman of prayer, spending about 2–3 hours a day on her knees, now she spent more time praying than ever before.

The diagnosis of my wife's condition also changed *my* life drastically. There was a definite change in my relationship with Becky. I became more gentle and understanding. Whereas I was in the past impatient with her and sometimes unwilling to put up with her weaknesses, I started noticing more her efforts to allow the Holy Spirit to transform her. Things I had missed before about her became very evident and clear. I called home more frequently when I was out of town. I was told she was dying in a few months, and I didn't want to hasten the process. Faced with the threat of death, I knew I didn't want to lose my wife. I wanted desperately for her to live, and my whole life then became riveted on that need.

My attitude towards my children even changed, especially as I kept wondering about whether or not I should break the tragic news to them. I started seeing our two children differently, for the first time seeing more clearly their mother's unique traits in them. I asked myself, "Who will take care of these children when their mother is gone?"

You would, perhaps, not understand what I'm talking about, unless you've experienced such a shattering wake-up call. If you have, you'd realize that many things that in the past had meant much to you suddenly have no value.

Wake-up calls do, indeed, change the way people look at themselves, at others, and at life in general.

> WAKE-UP CALLS DO, INDEED, CHANGE THE WAY
> PEOPLE LOOK AT THEMSELVES, AT OTHERS,
> AND AT LIFE IN GENERAL.

In the days after my wife's diagnosis, we slowly started considering our options: chemotherapy, surgery, natural remedies, etc. We read as much as we could on her condition. We later went to the hospital again for a follow-up examination so we would know what we needed to do right away. After another series of tests, the doctor announced to us that the cancer was gone!!

The doctor suggested that most likely the first diagnosis was a false one! (Well, I believe it was a miracle. God intervened in our behalf in this instance.) Years later, my wife would continue having brushes with cancer. But what *a gracious relief* it was on this particular occasion!

But notice what has happened to you, even upon hearing of my wife's "terminal" cancer. Most of you don't know my wife. I'm the only one you know. And yet, upon hearing the news, your attitude towards her changed.

I'm sure that your attitude towards me also changed. Even if for some reason you don't like me—or you even hate me because of my Bible-based positions and uncompromising stand against fashionable theological fads intruding into our church—the news I just narrated of my wife's impending death suddenly made you a little more sympathetic towards me. *Such should be our attitude towards one another at all times.*

You see, wake-up calls, regardless of who receives them, have a way of changing people around them.

Brothers and sisters, the tragic events in our world today should be wake-up calls for all of us. As such, they should fundamentally change the way we conduct our lives and relate to others. For the simple fact is that every one of us is terminally ill. We've been infected by a deadly cancer virus called sin, and this virus is going to kill us. If we understand this reality, perhaps our attitude towards others will change. We can be a little more forgiving and understanding. Then we shall start focusing on things that really matter, and we shall seek to anchor our hopes on that which is eternal.

It is against this background that I'd like to address the topic, "Where is your hope?"

We live in a post-9-11 world, a world that is witnessing an unprecedented series of challenges in our nation and around the world: issues of security and the erosion of fundamental personal liberty, religious intolerance and bigotry, questions of separation of church and state, economic woes, unemployment, hostility towards illegal immigrants, etc. All these are wake-up calls that should challenge us to reconsider our business-as-usual approach to life and spirituality.

Wake-up calls within our churches should also challenge us in the way we take our faith into our personal and corporate lives. For example, we must seriously reconsider the way some of us do "youth ministry" or conduct our worship services. Instead of the frivolity and entertainment that often masquerades as "worship innovation," we must begin to take God more seriously.

This is why I intend to speak candidly with you, drawing upon some real experiences I have witnessed. I've entitled the message today, "Where Is Your Hope?" It is a profound question that was first posed by the prophet Job. I trust that as we reflect on this question, you will reconsider the direction of your own life.

WHERE IS YOUR HOPE?[1]

Let's take a look at the origin of this question in Job 17:13–16 in the KJV:

> If I wait, the grave is mine house: I have made my bed in the darkness. I have said to corruption, Thou art my father: to the worm, Thou art my mother, and my sister. And where is now my hope? as for my hope, who shall see it? They shall go down to the bars of the pit, when our rest together is in the dust.

To get the force of the passage, let's compress the verses in the same KJV as follows:

> If I wait, the grave is mine house... And where is now my hope?
> (JOB 17:13A, 15A)

Some other Bible translations press home the point of the same question:

> If I look for Sheol as my home ... where now is my hope? (NASB)

> If the only home I hope for is the grave ... where then is my hope? (NIV)

If death or the grave is our inevitable end, where is our hope? If after you obtain an impressive academic degree, you secure a good job, purchase a comfortable car, home, etc., marry the most beautiful person, have lovely kids, ...—if after doing all these you die, then where is your hope?

Today, I want to pose to you Job's question by asking you: "Where Is Your Hope?" I'm asking you about your hope, because without hope there can be no meaningful life.

Hope is the most important ingredient of life. You may have heard the saying that *while there is life, there's always hope. But in the Bible the deeper truth is that while there is hope, there is life. Without hope, there is no life.*

A life without hope is like being in a tunnel that has no light at the end of it, only deeper darkness and eventually a blank wall. When we come to that point in our lives when we think or feel that we have nothing to hope for (in our studies, relationships, finances, or health) and can only expect things to get worse in the future, we inevitably grow depressed, and, to a degree, desperate. The desperation and depression resulting from the absence of hope can result in bitterness, rage, and hatred of life. And in some cases, when there is a feeling that all hope is gone, such a feeling leads people to commit suicide.

This is why the word "HOPELESS" is written across the details of almost every suicide or murder-suicide. If the word is not found in a note, we can still read it between the lines. Life without hope is not worth living. At the very best, such a life is reduced to a mere shadow existence.

This is why I raise again the serious question, "Where Is Your Hope?" It is a question I have asked many different student groups and church congregations. And I want you to give serious thought to this same question.

Notice that the question is not, *"What is your hope?"* I'm not asking you about the *object* of your hope. Rather, the question is, "Where is your hope?" I'm inquiring about the *foundation* or *source* of your hope. Do you have a solid foundation for your hope?

> IT IS SAID THAT WHILE THERE IS LIFE, THERE'S ALWAYS HOPE. BUT IN THE BIBLE THE DEEPER TRUTH IS THAT WHILE THERE IS HOPE, THERE IS LIFE. WITHOUT HOPE, THERE IS NO LIFE.

HOPE, NOT WISHFUL THINKING OR MERE OPTIMISM

Without a secured foundation, our so-called hope is *only wishful thinking*. At best, such a hope would be nothing more than a mere expression of optimism.

Unfortunately, this is how the dictionary defines hope. Notice the following definitions:

The word "hope" can be both a noun and a verb. *The American Heritage®
Dictionary of the English Language*, 4th edition, defines the noun "hope"
in this way:

- 1. TO WISH FOR SOMETHING WITH EXPECTATION
  OF ITS FULFILLMENT.
- 2. ARCHAIC. TO HAVE CONFIDENCE; TRUST.

The verb "to hope" means:

- 1. TO LOOK FORWARD TO WITH CONFIDENCE OR EXPECTATION:
  WE HOPE THAT OUR CHILDREN WILL BE SUCCESSFUL.
- 2. TO EXPECT AND DESIRE.

Similarly, *Webster's Revised Unabridged Dictionary* defines hope as:

A desire of some good, accompanied with an expectation of obtaining
it, or a belief that it is obtainable; an expectation of something which is
thought to be desirable; confidence; pleasing expectancy.

It appears to me, from the above dictionary definitions, that for many
people hope is nothing more than a "wish" or expectation for something
favorable. At the very best, it is a strong expression of optimism in a future
situation: a kind of "positive thinking."

WHERE IS THE FOUNDATION OF YOUR HOPE?

But you see, Job's question, "*Where* is your hope?" is more than a wish list
or something you are optimistic about. There is a great difference between
a "general feeling that what is wanted will happen" and the *grounds*, the
positive assurance that the expectation will actually happen.

Optimism about some prospects without any guarantee that we would
ever arrive at the object of our hope is *delusional* or *crazy*.

It's like saying, "I know I will marry a billionaire one day" (Dream on!
You don't even know you will ever get married, let alone marry a billionaire).

Or it's like hearing someone say, "I'll be in Med School next year to become a neurosurgeon" (Really? When you're getting Cs, Ds, and Fs in your biology and chemistry classes today? Wake up!).

Or even saying "I'll be the CEO of a Fortune 500 company by the end of next year" (Interesting! When you've never learned how to do an honest day's work?).

You say you'll have a great family with a loving spouse and kids who will grow up to be responsible? And you don't even care what happens to them now? Get real and don't be delusional!

Sadly, much of contemporary Christianity has also bought into this delusional theology of hope. Anchored in thin air, this groundless "hope" is built on positive-thinking "faith" (devoid of any living connection with Christ), dressed up in a Biblically unsatisfying "belief in Jesus," and advertised and sold in clone versions of "Whatever you conceive and *believe*, you can *achieve*." Let's wake up from our stupor! Even a little teaspoon of Bible knowledge can easily overthrow our "success formula" Christianity.

There are no grounds for these wishes or beliefs. Therefore, the expression of such a "hope" is simply crazy or delusional. Marxist philosophers refer to such a hope as "a pie in the sky when you die." It is building "castles in the air." And some psychological counselors call this kind of hope "escapism"—keeping people from facing the realities of life.

Job's question, "Where is your hope?" is a call to root hope in a secured foundation. If the foundation is strong, the structure will be solid. When the tree of hope is firmly rooted and nourished, the desired fruits will be forthcoming.

On the other hand, when the foundation of our hope is shaky, in times of crisis we cannot truly live or even merely survive. Our hopes will be dashed and shattered when they are anchored on shifting sand.

> SADLY, MUCH OF CONTEMPORARY CHRISTIANITY HAS ALSO BOUGHT INTO THIS DELUSIONAL THEOLOGY OF HOPE.

If, for example, we place our hope in *human beings*, what would happen when those individuals, whether they be friends, family, etc., fail us or die? When our hopes are rooted in the wrong things, where would be our hope? Where would be our hope ...

~ when our sources of livelihood (our job, business, bank account, etc.) are suddenly lost?

~ when our prospects of a meaningful happy future are shattered (by our boyfriend/girlfriend, fiancé/fiancée, husband, wife)?

~ when our educational degree lets us down (e.g., when we fail our exams or job interviews)?

~ when our self-worth dissolves into self-doubt, self-distrust, and self-dislike?

~ when we are diagnosed with fatal diseases like cancer, AIDS, etc.?

~ when sudden death strikes very close to us through an accident, plane crash, heart attack, stray bullets?

MY MEETING WITH THERESA

I started thinking seriously about Job's question several years ago, while I was living in Berrien Springs, Michigan. One early Wednesday morning, I got a call from Chicago urging me to come down immediately. The reason? A very close friend of mine, who had been greatly impacted by my ministry, was dying. Theresa became a dear sister to me, and she viewed me as her "personal pastor."

Different people or groups address me in different ways, with each appellation revealing the level of our relationship. Some call me "Pipim," "Dr. Pipim," or "Pastor Pipim." To others, I'm "Samuel," "Sam," "Uncle," "Sammy," or "Dr. P." My classmates from my student days in Ghana call me by another special name (which I will not reveal here). I can almost predict how close individuals are to me by how they address me. For Theresa, I was "My Pastor," because I was her "personal pastor." But if she were in a really gloomy mood, she would simply address me as "Pastor." And now she was dying.

It was the father who placed the call. He explained that Theresa had terminal breast cancer and had been brought home to die. While the family was doing everything they could for her, the father explained that Theresa had become withdrawn, angry, and upset with everyone. She would not even talk with her parents, her husband, or her church pastor. Her father reasoned that because I was very close to her, perhaps I could help.

I rushed to Chicago that morning. Upon arrival, I noticed that the atmosphere in the home was eerie and tense, almost as though a plague of death had hit the family. After exchanging a few words of greetings in whispered tones, Theresa's parents pointed me to the room where Theresa lay.

I entered the room, not knowing what to expect. Her facial expression suggested to me that she was relieved to see me, although I could tell she was in great pain. She slowly lifted herself up, and then without any kind of preliminary remarks, she asked me pointedly: "Pastor, am I going to die?"

I was not prepared for that unexpected question. In what seemed to me like eternity, I fumbled for an appropriate answer: "What kind of question is this you are asking, Theresa? You haven't even acknowledged my presence with the traditional welcome greeting, and you are asking me this tough question."

But she was insistent: "It's an important question to me. Am I going to die?"

"Theresa, only God knows the answer to this kind of question, and I am not God," I carefully tried to answer.

But she still remained adamant. Her facial expression and subsequent words indicated that she was in no mood for that kind of answer: "Pastor, I highly respect you. And I want an honest answer from you. Tell me, am I going to die? If you won't answer this question candidly, I'll invite you to leave this room immediately!"

"Well, if you demand a candid answer, I will tell you. It appears from what I see lying before me that you are dying—unless God supernaturally intervenes," I responded.

At my answer, Theresa smiled!—an action that left me startled and even more confused. Then she explained,

"My Pastor, this is why I respect you. You are one of the few people I trust. You say exactly what is on your mind, and are not afraid to speak the truth—even unpopular and unpleasant truth. And you've just confirmed my respect for your integrity. You see, you are the only one who has had the courage to tell me the truth about my condition.

"I know that I am dying. The doctors also know it. Yet almost everyone who comes here to visit me tries to convince me that I am going to live. They say all kinds of things to assure me that because they have fasted and prayed for me, God *will* answer their prayers by restoring me to life. But how do they know the mind of God? It almost seems to me that they are trying to force or command God to heal me.

"After putting up with this kind of presumption for some time, I concluded that they are all a bunch of liars. And I determined that the last few days that the Lord will spare my life, I don't want liars to surround me. I'd prefer to die only in the company of real Christians, and if I can't find them I would rather choose to die alone, all by myself—even if I have to be alone. This is why I do not want to see my parents, husband, or even pastor. I'm very angry with them."

"OK, Theresa, if you know you're dying, what preparations have you made? Do you think an angry person will experience the resurrection when Jesus comes to take His children—the living who are alive and the resurrected saints—with Him to Heaven?"

This question led Theresa and me into a lively, but solemn, discussion of hope. We talked about the Christian's assurance of salvation and the need for her to make things right with those around her (Theresa subsequently made things right with her family and pastor).

We also discussed what she'd like to see done when she died—who should take care of her two children, who should conduct and take part in her funeral, how she should be dressed up in her casket or coffin, the hymns and Scripture to be selected, where she should be buried, etc.

After a candid dialogue, we reviewed some familiar promises from God's Word. I wish I could transport you to that room to listen in to our conversation. For then you would see how a Christian dies!

We reviewed the Bible's teaching about death, showing that regardless of how a person dies, it is comforting to know that *death is only a sleep.* I said

IF YOU KNOW YOU'RE DYING, WHAT PREPARATIONS HAVE YOU MADE?

to her, "Theresa, you'll be OK. After all the pain and suffering from this illness, you will be laid to sleep—no more suffering and pain."

I reminded her of some well-known Bible characters, how they all "fell asleep" in death, though the manner of their deaths were all different:

~ Abel asleep (after being violently killed by his brother Cain); GENESIS 4

~ Some 18 church members in Jerusalem asleep (after the accident in the church, when the tower fell and killed them); LUKE 13:1–5

~ Lazarus asleep (after illness); JOHN 11:11

~ Stephen slept (after the torture of being stoned); ACTS 7:60

~ David asleep (after old age; cf. Moses, Jacob, etc.); ACTS 2:29, 34

~ Old Testament martyrs asleep (after being sawn asunder, burned, drowned, etc.) HEBREWS. 11:35–40

Though all these died in different ways, today, *they are all asleep* (PETER DECLARES THIS OF DAVID: ACTS 2:22–29), experiencing no more pain or hurt. Death, according to the Bible, is not a separate existence somewhere else. It is a complete cessation of life, not a continuation of life in a location with a different ZIP code address (Heaven, Hell, purgatory, ghostland, etc.). *Death is sleep.*

But how long will they be sleeping? Is there no time when they will wake up from their sleep?

Theresa and I reviewed the Biblical teaching that showed that they will continue sleeping until Jesus comes to wake them up. For example, the patriarch Job asked:

> But man dies and is laid away;
> Indeed he breathes his last
> And where is he?
> As water disappears from the sea,
> And a river becomes parched and dries up,
> So man lies down and does not rise.
> Till the heavens are no more,
> They will not awake
> Nor be roused from their sleep.
> "Oh, that You would hide me in the grave,
> That You would conceal me until Your wrath is past,
> That You would appoint me a set time, and remember me!
> If a man dies, shall he live again?
> All the days of my hard service I will wait,
> Till my change comes.
> You shall call, and I will answer You;
> You shall desire the work of Your hands"
>
> (JOB 14:10–15).

Those who die or sleep in the Lord will wake up one day when Jesus comes. When "the heavens are no more," when the Lord will "call and we will answer." The dead are sleeping quietly in their graves until Jesus comes to resurrect them—some to eternal life and others to eternal damnation.

Here's what our Lord Himself stated:

> "And this is the will of Him Who sent Me, that everyone who sees the Son and believes in Him may have everlasting life; and I will raise him up at the last day" (JOHN 6:40).

> "Most assuredly, I say to you, the hour is coming, and now is, when the dead will hear the voice of the Son of God; and those who hear will live. Do not marvel at this; for the hour is coming in which all who are in the graves will hear His voice and come forth—those who have

done good, to the resurrection of life, and those who have done evil, to the resurrection of condemnation" (JOHN 5:25, 28, 29).

The apostle Paul also wrote:

> For if we believe that Jesus died and rose again, even so God will bring with Him those who sleep in Jesus. For this we say to you by the word of the Lord, that we who are alive and remain until the coming of the Lord will by no means precede those who are asleep. For the Lord Himself will descend from Heaven with a shout, with the voice of an Archangel, and with the trumpet of God. And the dead in Christ will rise first. Then we who are alive and remain shall be caught up together with them in the clouds to meet the Lord in the air. And thus we shall always be with the Lord. Therefore comfort one another with these words (1 THESSALONIANS 4:14–18).

Writing to the Corinthians, Paul also wrote:

> Behold, I tell you a mystery: We shall not all sleep, but we shall all be changed—in a moment, in the twinkling of an eye, at the last trumpet. For the trumpet will sound, and the dead will be raised incorruptible, and we shall be changed. For this corruptible must put on incorruption, and this mortal must put on immortality. So when this corruptible has put on incorruption, and this mortal has put on immortality, then shall be brought to pass the saying that is written: "Death is swallowed up in victory."
> "O Death, where is your sting?
> O Hades, where is your victory?"
> (1 CORINTHIANS 15:51–55).

I wish you could have been in that room with me as Theresa and I read these familiar Bible passages. On the authority of the Word of God, I assured her that it is a blessing to die in the Lord, for there is hope beyond the grave.

Death is the ultimate failure: failure of our health and failure of our earthly lives. But we need not be afraid of death because there is hope beyond the grave. *There is hope beyond ultimate failure.*

If we have a living connection with God, we need not fear death—this ultimate failure in life. On the contrary, we can face death with confidence; for the Bible tells us that the death of the child of God is precious in His sight. Though we naturally are sad at the loss of our loved ones, death is not the end. If they died in Christ, they'll live again. What a precious thought! No wonder the Bible says, "Precious in the eyes of the Lord is the death of His saints" (PSALM 116:15).

"Then I heard a voice from Heaven saying to me, 'Write: "Blessed are the dead who die in the Lord from now on."'" "Yes," says the Spirit, "that they may rest from their labors, and their works follow them" (REVELATION 14:13).

"And God will wipe away every tear from their eyes; there shall be no more death, nor sorrow, nor crying. There shall be no more pain, for the former things have passed away" (REVELATION 21:4).

Oh, I wish you could be there to watch a Bible-knowing and believing Christian die. These Bible passages take on a whole new meaning when you stare death in the face.

Anyway, Theresa and I encouraged ourselves in the Lord. She resigned fully to God's will regarding whether to heal her or not. She knew God cannot fail. "There's no failure *with* God." The operative word there is "with God." Those who have a living connection with Him, those who abide in Christ, need not worry about their future.

Thus Theresa readied herself to die—if that was God's will for her life. *She surrendered her life to God* by deciding to allow God to have the final say about her life. Like Christ in the Garden of Gethsemane, she also said in her own words: "Father, if You are willing, take this cup from me; *yet not my will, but Yours be done*" (LUKE 22:42).

When Theresa thus surrendered to God, she also received strength from the Lord. (In the case of Christ, we are told, "An angel from Heaven appeared to Him and *strengthened Him*" (V. 43). No angel appeared to Theresa that day, but the Holy Spirit Himself was in the room to comfort and encourage her to face this ultimate failure of life: death—if that was God's will for her at that time.

We parted company that Wednesday in very good spirits. I promised to be back the next Sabbath (i.e., Saturday) to see her. But early Friday morning her parents called to say her condition had worsened and that she had therefore been taken back to the hospital.

I rushed to Chicago again that Friday. At the hospital, surrounded by her immediate family, I took her by the hand and said, "Theresa, it's me. If you can hear my voice, give me a little squeeze."

I'm not sure she did, although in my mind I felt she did. Anyway, in the presence of the family, I reminded her of those Bible promises we had read two days earlier. I assured her that if her life was hidden in Christ, if she abode in Him, we shall see her again on the resurrection morning when Jesus comes back to take His children home to Heaven.

We sang some good hymns (like "It Is Well With My Soul," etc.), and a few minutes later she died quietly.

> IF WE HAVE A LIVING CONNECTION WITH GOD, WE NEED NOT FEAR DEATH—THIS ULTIMATE FAILURE IN LIFE.

STRONG DOUBTS

As we finalized her funeral arrangements, Theresa's parents asked me to take her little children to the funeral home so they could see their mother for the last time before her burial. It was a most sobering experience for me. But what happened there is something I will never forget.

The body was in the casket and the children didn't seem to understand what had happened. I stood quietly as I gazed at the face of Theresa. A few days earlier, she had blood flowing through her veins. Now she was still. Not long ago, she was full of life–even in her illness. She showed human emotions as we laughed, cried, and sang. But now she was still, and the very color of her skin betrayed the fact that she was truly dead.

If you've never seen your loved one's cold, lifeless frame, you may not fully understand what I'm now discussing. Death is dreadful. Or as the Bible puts it, death is an enemy. That is why Jesus came to defeat death. That is why He holds the key to death (SEE REVELATION 1:18).

While beholding the lifeless remains of Theresa inside that casket, a strange thought suddenly struck me. It is a thought that literally *shook the foundation of my faith*.

It seemed as though some presence other than the two little kids was present in that room with me (I want to believe it was some evil spirits, trying to whisper doubt in my mind). I heard what seemed like a voice ask me these haunting questions:

> *"What if you lied to Theresa? What if all you shared with her were not true? What if there is no Second Coming? What if there is no resurrection? What if the Bible is not true?"*

I cannot describe to you the dread that came upon me when those words of doubt were urged upon me. In what seemed like a long time, my faith in God and the Bible started giving way. During that moment of strong doubt, all that saved my faith were the following words from the apostle Paul:

> Now if Christ is preached that He has been raised from the dead, how do some among you say that there is no resurrection of the dead? But if there is no resurrection of the dead, *then Christ is not risen. And if Christ is not risen, then our preaching is empty and your faith is also empty. Yes, and we are found false witnesses of God*, because we have testified of God that He raised up Christ, Whom He did not raise up—if in fact the dead do not rise. For if the dead do not rise, *then Christ is not risen.* And if Christ is not risen, *your faith is futile; you are still in your sins! Then also those who have fallen asleep in Christ have perished.* If in this life only we have hope in Christ, *we are of all men the most pitiable.* But now Christ is risen from the dead, and has become the Firstfruits of those who have fallen asleep. For since by man came death, by Man also came the resurrection of the dead. If, in the manner of men, I have fought with beasts at Ephesus, what advantage is it to me? If the dead do not rise, *"Let us eat and drink, for tomorrow we die!"* (1 CORINTHIANS 15:12-21, 32).

Those words became the foundation of my hope during that moment of intense doubt. No, I did not lie to Theresa. The Bible passages I shared with her were true. There is going to be a Second Coming of Christ. There will be a resurrection. The Bible is true. How do I know? *Because Jesus rose again.* We serve a risen Savior. And this fact is the foundation of our hope.

The apostle Paul says that without such a foundation we might as well "eat and drink, for tomorrow we die" (1 CORINTHIANS 15:32). We might as well adopt the ethics of Epicureanism or hedonism. In other words, our world-view determines our ethics.

If we don't have a hope beyond the grave—if we don't have hope beyond ultimate failure—we are the most miserable bunch of people. Our lives are no different from the poultry chicken that lives, eats, dies, ... and that's it! Our fate is no different, then, from the skunk that winds up as roadkill.

But if there is hope beyond the grave—hope beyond ultimate failure—then we can't live anyhow. If there is a Second Coming and a Judgment Day ahead, when everyone will be rewarded according as his works shall be, then we must begin to live a different kind of life. Our lifestyle—what we eat, drink, wear, watch, etc., will all be determined by what will glorify God (SEE 1 CORINTHIANS 10:31).

My question to you is, *"Do you have this hope?"* Do you have a reason for the [Christian] hope?"

THE CHRISTIAN HOPE

Whereas unbelievers are without this hope (EPHESIANS 2:12; 1 THESSALONIANS 4:13), the Bible teaches that the Christian's life is centered in hope (EPHESIANS 1:18; 4:4)—a "lively" (i.e., a living) hope, a hope not frail and perishable, but having a perennial life (1 PETER 1:3). Let's briefly summarize the nature of this hope:

1. GOD IS THE SOURCE OF HOPE.

"May the God of hope fill you with all joy and peace as you trust in Him, so that you may overflow with hope by the power of the Holy Spirit" (ROMANS 15:13).

"The Lord will be the hope of His people" (JOEL 3:16).

"For Thou art my hope, O Lord God: Thou art my trust from my youth" (PSALM 71:5).

2. CHRIST IS HIMSELF OUR HOPE (BECOMING AT HIS INCARNATION THE MESSENGER OF HOPE).

"Christ Jesus [is] our hope" (1 TIMOTHY 1:1);

"Christ in you, [is] the hope of glory" (COLOSSIANS 1:27; CF. TITUS 2:13).

3. THE CHRISTIAN HOPE BRINGS JOY.

"We rejoice in the hope of the glory of God" (ROMANS 5:2);

"Be joyful in hope" (ROMANS 12:12).

4. THE CHRISTIAN HOPE BRINGS PATIENCE.

"For in this hope we are saved. But hope that is seen is no hope at all. Who hopes for what he already has? But if we hope for what we do not yet have, we wait for it patiently" (ROMANS 8:24, 25);

"All things work together for good ..." (V. 28).

5. THE CHRISTIAN HOPE IS LINKED WITH FAITH.

Hebrews 11:1 defines faith in terms of hope: "Now faith is the substance of things hoped for, the evidence of things not seen". The NIV puts it this way: "Now faith is being sure of what we hope for and certain of what we do not see."

6. THE SECOND COMING IS THE CONSUMMATION OF TTHE CHRISTIAN HOPE.

It is the blessed hope. Such a hope lives beyond the grave and will be made manifest when Christ appears in the clouds of glory to redeem His own. This is the ultimate security of our hope. The apostle Paul refers to it as "the blessed hope": "Looking for that blessed hope, and the glorious appearing of the great God and our Saviour Jesus Christ" (TITUS 2:13).

7. THE CHRISTIAN HOPE BELIEVES IN THE PROMISES OF GOD.

It is the kind of hope Abraham had. Because he believed that God was shaping his future, we are told: "Against all hope, Abraham in hope believed … being fully persuaded that God had a power to do what He had promised" (ROMANS 4:1–3, 16–22).

8. CONVERSION IS THE WAY WE ARRIVE AT CHRISTIAN HOPE.

"Praise be to the God and Father of our Lord Jesus Christ! In His great mercy He has given us new birth into a living hope through the resurrection of Jesus Christ from the death, and into an inheritance that can never perish, spoil or fade …" (1 PETER 1:3–9).

9. SCRIPTURES ARE THE MEANS TO OBTAIN AND SUSTAIN THE CHRISTIAN HOPE.

"For whatsoever things were written aforetime were written for our learning, that we through patience and comfort of the Scriptures might have hope" (ROMANS 15:4).

10. THE CHRISTIAN HOPE IS SECURELY GROUNDED IN A LIVING SAVIOR.

Because it is anchored in a living Savior, the Christian hope is solidly grounded. "Which hope we have as an anchor of the soul, both sure and steadfast, and which entereth into that within the veil" (HEBREWS 6:19; CF. 1 PETER 1:3).

11. THE CHRISTIAN HOPE GOVERNS OUR LIFE TODAY.

"And every man that hath this hope in him purifieth himself, even as He is pure" (1 JOHN 3:3);

"Seeing then that all these things shall be dissolved, what manner of persons ought ye to be in all holy conversation and godliness, looking for and hasting unto the coming of the day of God, wherein the heavens being on fire shall be dissolved, and the elements shall melt with fervent heat? Nevertheless we, according to His promise, look for new heavens and a new earth, wherein dwelleth righteousness. Wherefore, beloved, seeing that ye look for such things, be diligent that ye may be found of Him in peace, without spot, and blameless" (2 PETER 3:11-14).

〜 12. THE CHRISTIAN HOPE IS A LIVING HOPE THAT ISSUES FROM GOD'S ABUNDANT MERCY.

"Blessed be the God and Father of our Lord Jesus Christ, Who according to His abundant mercy has begotten us again to a living hope through the resurrection of Jesus Christ from the dead, to an inheritance incorruptible and undefiled and that does not fade away, reserved in Heaven for you, who are kept by the power of God through faith for salvation ready to be revealed in the last time.... Therefore gird up the loins of your mind, be sober, and rest your hope fully upon the grace that is to be brought to you at the revelation of Jesus Christ" (1 PETER 1:3-5, 13).

The above elements of the Christian hope are the basis for the Christian's belief that there is hope beyond ultimate failure—a certainty of hope beyond the grave.

JOB'S HOPE BEYOND THE GRAVE

We began our study with the question posed by Job:

"If the only home I hope for is the grave ... where then is my hope?" (JOB 17:13A, 15A, NIV)

Where is our hope beyond the grave—beyond ultimate failure? It is worthy of note that two chapters after Job asked the question, "Where Is My Hope?" he provided an answer for us. After recounting how everything he once treasured had failed him: his friends, acquaintances, kinsfolk, wife, health, etc. (JOB 19:13–20), he stated confidently:

> For I know that my Redeemer lives,
> And He shall stand at last on the earth;
> And after my skin is destroyed, this I know,
> That in my flesh I shall see God,
> Whom I shall see for myself,
> And my eyes shall behold, and not another.
> How my heart yearns within me!"
>
> (JOB 19: 25–27).

"For I know …" (that is certainty). "I know my Redeemer lives" (that is the ground of our hope). The foundation of the believer's hope is a risen Savior. "My Redeemer lives." In the words of the familiar song in our hymnbook:

> I serve a risen Saviour; He's in the world today.
> I know that He is living, whatever men may say.
> I see His hand of mercy, I hear His voice of cheer,
> And just the time I need Him He's always near.

Chorus:

> *He lives! He lives! Christ Jesus lives today!*
> *He walks with me and talks with me along life's narrow way.*
> *He lives! He lives! Salvation to impart!*
> *You ask me how I know He lives? He lives within my heart.*

> In all the world around me I see His loving care,
> And though my heart grows weary I never will despair.
> I know that He is leading, thro' all the stormy blast;
> The day of His appearing will come at last.

> Rejoice, rejoice, O Christian! Lift up your voice and sing
> Eternal hallelujahs to Jesus Christ, the King!

The Hope of all who seek Him, the Help of all who find,
None other is so loving, so good and kind.

The Biblical hope is a certainty, guaranteed by God Himself. It is rooted in the fact that Jesus lives. That certainty says, "I know my redeemer lives." It is the kind of hope that leads the believer in God to say with Job, "Though He slay me, yet will I trust in Him" (JOB 13:15).

It is that kind of hope that can look in the eyes of danger and still proclaim: "Our God Whom we serve is able to deliver us from the burning fiery furnace, and He will deliver us from your hand, O king. But if not, let it be known to you, O king, that we do not serve your gods, nor will we worship the gold image which you have set up" (DANIEL 3:17, 18).

The Biblical hope can offer certainty, on the basis of God's own commitment, that the best is yet to come:

"And we know that all things work together for good to those who love God, to those who are the called according to His purpose.... Who shall separate us from the love of Christ? Shall tribulation, or distress, or persecution, or famine, or nakedness, or peril, or sword? ... Yet in all these things we are more than conquerors through Him Who loved us. For I am persuaded that neither death nor life, nor angels nor principalities nor powers, nor things present nor things to come, nor height nor depth, nor any other created thing, shall be able to separate us from the love of God which is in Christ Jesus our Lord" (ROMANS 8:28, 35, 37–39).

HOPE FOR THE BEREAVED

Just in case you have lost a loved one, permit me to share with you a comforting statement from the writings of Ellen G. White about this Biblical hope. The statement concerns the "Blessed Hope" of the resurrection:

All that has perplexed us in the providences of God will in the world to come be made plain. The things hard to be understood will then find explanation. The mysteries of grace will unfold before us. Where our finite minds discovered only confusion and broken promises, we shall see the most perfect and beautiful harmony. We shall know that Infinite

Love ordered the experiences that seemed most trying. As we realize the tender care of Him Who makes all things work together for our good, we shall rejoice with joy unspeakable and full of glory.

Pain cannot exist in the atmosphere of Heaven. In the home of the redeemed there will be no tears, no funeral trains, no badges of mourning. "The inhabitant shall not say, I am sick: the people that dwell therein shall be forgiven their iniquity." (ISAIAH 33:24). One rich tide of happiness will flow and deepen as eternity rolls on.

> THE BIBLICAL HOPE IS A CERTAINTY,
> GUARANTEED BY GOD HIMSELF.
> IT IS ROOTED IN THE FACT THAT JESUS LIVES.
> THAT CERTAINTY SAYS,
> "I KNOW MY REDEEMER LIVES."

We are still amidst the shadows and turmoil of earthly activities. Let us consider most earnestly the blessed hereafter. Let our faith pierce through every cloud of darkness and behold Him Who died for the sins of the world. He has opened the gates of Paradise to all who receive and believe on Him. To them He gives power to become the sons and daughters of God. Let the afflictions which pain us so grievously become instructive lessons, teaching us to press forward toward the mark of the prize of our high calling in Christ. Let us be encouraged by the thought that the Lord is soon to come. Let this hope gladden our hearts....

We are homeward bound. He Who loved us so much as to die for us hath builded for us a city. The New Jerusalem is our place of rest. There will be no sadness in the City of God. No wail of sorrow, no dirge of crushed hopes and buried affections, will evermore be heard. Soon the garments of heaviness will be changed for the wedding garment.

Soon we shall witness the coronation of our King. Those whose lives have been hidden with Christ, those who on this earth have fought the good fight of faith, will shine forth with the Redeemer's glory in the Kingdom of God.

> DEATH IS NOT THE WORST THING THAT COULD HAPPEN TO ANYONE. THE WORST THAT CAN HAPPEN IS DEATH WITHOUT CHRIST. THAT IS ULTIMATE FAILURE.

It will not be long till we shall see Him in Whom our hopes of eternal life are centered. And in His presence, all the trials and sufferings of this life will be as nothingness. "Cast not away therefore your confidence, which hath great recompense of reward. For ye have need of patience, that, after ye have done the will of God, ye might receive the promise. For yet a little while, and He that shall come will come, and will not tarry" (HEBREWS 10:35–37). Look up, look up, and let your faith continually increase. Let this faith guide you along the narrow path that leads through the gates of the City of God into the great beyond, the wide, unbounded future glory that is for the redeemed. "Be patient therefore, brethren, unto the coming of the Lord. Behold, the husbandman waiteth for the precious fruit of the earth, and hath long patience for it, until he receive the early and latter rain. Be ye also patient; stablish your hearts: for the coming of the Lord draweth nigh." (JAMES 5:7, 8.2)

May we all be comforted by these words as we ground our faith in our living Savior, Who will soon come for His own. There is hope beyond the grave. There is hope beyond ultimate failure. Death is not the end. There is a resurrection.

Death is not the worst thing that could happen to anyone. The worst that can happen is death *without Christ*. That is ultimate failure. But with Christ, there is hope beyond ultimate failure.

Since God has given us assurance of hope beyond ultimate failure, why shouldn't we believe that there can be success in the midst of our many failures in life?

A NOTE TO THE READER

The very day I was completing this chapter, I received a note from a dear friend of mine. He's one of the few individuals who personally ministered to me during the trying ordeals of my spiritual failure. Dr. Leroy Moore is a retired theology professor and pastor.

From his own pain and that of his terminally ill wife Pat, the Lord equipped Dr. Moore to minister to me in my pain—a pain resulting from the consequences of sin: my sin. From the moment he heard of the tragedy of my spiritual failure, he drew much closer to me and literally offered himself and assumed the role as MY personal pastor, teacher, mentor, and friend.

From him I learned that pain is not merely the price of sin, but investment in righteousness. For it is in facing the painful results of sin that God prepares us for the rich blessings of His righteousness.

Armed with this new insight into pain, I determined to let my reflections on failure be a source of character transformation. And Dr. Leroy Moore was with me every step of the way, as I worked through the pain, shame, hurt—from both foes and friends. He also provided the most extensive input into my thinking about lessons from my failure.

As if this chapter was written for him, just after I sent the draft, he quickly e-mailed this back to me:

> *"I have spent the last five and a half hours with my wife who is in most intense pain. We have been unable to find any way to relieve the pain. We think she might be getting close to the end. God is good and her faith has been stable. Pray with us for her relief from pain."*

Then, after he subsequently got to read this present chapter, he responded:

My dear Brother Samuel,

I am so grateful for this opportunity to thank you for this wonderful and most appropriate section of your book which converges with my own experience in parting—for a short time—from my most precious possession. It is now a little after 4:30 AM. Though it was after midnight when I retired last night, I have been awake since 3:30 so decided to get up and respond to your message on hope beyond the grave.

It must have been near 11:00 Friday morning when I came to my office to send an urgent but very different message. But on arriving I found a couple of messages from you and briefly responded with the note you quote above regarding my wife's pain. I was about ready to return home the half block to Pat, without writing the other message, when my youngest granddaughter, Bethany ran in, exclaiming, "Grandpa, come quick, it's Grandma." I quickly ran home only to find that Pat's suffering was ended in peaceful sleep.

With the six hours of intense pain I had spent with her, which no pain medicine seemed to even touch, I had sensed that her end might be much nearer than the spring, to which we anticipated she would last. But I was wholly unprepared for such an immediate and final answer to our prayers, those in which my daughter Leanne and her husband had joined. As we saw her tortured by pain and all our efforts to relieve her pain were unavailing, we had been praying for her relief in the way God saw best.

What a shock! And how sorry I was to have been away at the very end. I wish I could have had a last prayer with her before she breathed her last. But I must testify, my Brother Samuel, that as intense as [was] my grief in losing her for the moment, even greater was my joy and intense sense of triumph as my dearest possession and friend on Earth passed forever beyond the reach of the enemy.

Indeed, I was compelled to exclaim through my tears, "She has fought a good fight. She has finished her course. She has kept the faith. Henceforth there is laid up for her a crown of righteousness, which the Lord, the righteous Judge, will give her on that day" (SEE 2 TIM. 4:7, 8). What a mixture of sorrow and joy. As intense as was (and is) the sorrow, it was (and is) overcome and overwhelmed by joy in knowing that Pat entered the safety zone of deep sleep where she can be tormented no more, to await "that day" when Christ will come and the trumpet will awaken her and unite us foreverv

What a terrible but blessed year 2011 proved. On January 1 Pat took seriously ill with pneumonia as a result of her almost nonexistent immune system caused by the chemotherapy she was undergoing. Before she could really recover from that, it became evident that she had a serious problem in her brain. Numerous tests, including four biopsies, finally ruled out cancer and identified five infectious lesions. After weeks of hospital and months of nursing home where she was treated with high-powered antibiotics, she was finally able to return home, after losing 60 pounds and hardly able to stand. As we provided green drinks and many nutritious herbs, her strength gradually began to return. But then, after one of her biweekly blood draws, her oncologist informed her that her routine blood sample, in preparation for another two pints of blood she had to undergo, had him concerned and that she must undergo another battery of blood tests.

It was a cruel report he had to give. She had been treated for a couple of years for a bone problem that prevented her blood cells to mature—thus the regular blood infusions were reaching a critical state because of the buildup of iron. When certain bad cells reach 20%, the diagnosis is full-blown leukemia. Pat's bad blood cells proved to be 45%.

That is a brief overview of the "terrible" part of the year. The blessed part is that God had prepared my wife, who had struggled with depression through the years, with a peace and tranquility that was a blessing to behold. When many months ago she followed the counsel of James 5:14, 15 and called for the elders to anoint her, she told them she did not want them to pray for her healing, but for God's will to be done. Throughout the year (we had not expected her to last till our 59th anniversary on June 8) she maintained complete trust in God. Though longing to be healed and doing all she knew to do to that end, she always wanted only God's will to be done. And when she went to sleep we praised Him for answering her (our) prayers.

How appropriate that the testimony she wanted to give in the church last Sabbath and which I gave for her, could come just as you were finishing the last section of your book and its focus upon "Beyond Ultimate Failure." The great failure proves to be that of the enemy of Christ and man who seeks to destroy faith in the Lifegiver by despair over his constant efforts to draw a black veil of despair over Christ's faithful children. He Who defeated him at the cross has triumphed once more. PRAISE THE LORD!

At the memorial service of Dr. Moore's wife the following Sabbath, a beautiful poem was read. Its author, Marvene Celeste Cabey-Jones, is a coworker of Dr. Moore at Weimar College, California. Her Poem, "Timeless

Life and Death," captures the Christian hope beyond the grave. The poem itself was written upon the death of one of its author's loved ones. With her permission, I am sharing it with readers of *Six More Chances*.

Timeless Life and Death

Within the womb the forming child is known,
The Master plans his triumph o'er his foes;
As screaming to this frightful world he goes,
From peaceful warmth to cold confusion he is thrown.

This fragile life begins—yet soon will end in death;
The sands of time will play uncertain games,
As rolling dice reveal unwelcome change,
In just one moment he could draw his final breath.

Yet ... He's in God's plan—a place that only he can fill,
O'er hills and valleys, although the river bends
There is a certain destiny at final journey's end,
For Life is timeless when you choose the Father's will.

See!!! The secret of a timeless life is daily death!
Will fears forbid our timid souls from tasting rest?
Will this man find the faith to take the test?
And sacrifice "dear self" for vital Holy Spirit's breath?

In triumph, mortal man completes the chosen way,
And solemn summons falls upon his ear so blessed;
That gentle voice had called him often times to rest,
As hourglass had marked the ending of each day.

He had no fear, for daily death had been a friend;
Its peace had been a welcome way of life,
He'd tasted rest and freedom from all strife.
And timeless life, now his, will have no bitter end!

He rests in peace and freedom from all pain,
'Til trumpet sounds to banish parting sore,
Immortal bodies rise to die no more,
The grave and death are conquered, victory's gained!

Don't weep for sleeping saints! Plead for your faithless soul
If daily death is not your timeless secret;
Your sands may cease to fall; your sun may set,
And prove that you're not closer to your goal.

God has a plan for you, a place that only you can fill,
Don't let fear forbid your timid soul from tasting rest!
Rise up and grasp the faith to pass the test,
For life is timeless when you choose the Father's will!

—*Marvene Celeste Cabey-Jones*
(10/6/2011 in honor of Raleigh Flint)

CHAPTER 4

⌣

THE KEY
TO SUCCESS

Six More Chances: Keep Getting Up
("M'akoma Ahye Ma")

Just as death is considered the ultimate failure in practical everyday life, spiritual failures—especially among religious people or those in positions of trust—are viewed as equally deadly.

Religious people (and sometimes nonreligious people) are prone to see certain misbehaviors in others as worse than their own. Ranking high within the categories of spiritual failures are "moral failures" (fornication, adultery, homosexuality, out-of-wedlock pregnancies, and all the various aberrations). They simply cannot imagine others ever falling morally or committing sins that are perceived to be more "repugnant" or to have greater consequences than their own failures that they deem inconsequential.

Thus, when these individuals hear of people who are exposed or who confess guilt in these areas, they are prone to think it can never happen to them. And the treatment suffered by people who have experienced spiritual failure within the religious community can be even more devastating than the pain from their fall. Sometimes the pain can be far worse than the pain of death itself.

EVERY SIN A MORAL FAILURE

If the truth be told, we've all experienced a "moral fall." No one is immune from spiritual failure. "All have sinned, and come short of the glory of God" (ROMANS 3:23), is the Biblical verdict. We have all experienced some "moral failure" because any time we violate any of the precepts in God's moral Law (the Ten Commandments or Decalogue), we have experienced a "moral fall."

Unfortunately, this fact is not always understood. We tend to think that only sexual sins are "moral failures." We deem selfishness, pride, jealousy, malice, covetousness, gossip, etc., to be more "respectable" sins than sexual ones. But the Bible is very clear that every sin, every violation of the Ten Commandments, is a moral failure. If we violate one of the moral laws, we've violated all.[1]

This lack of understanding of the "immoral" nature of every sin often leads us to consider those who have thus failed spiritually as being outcasts or rejects, forever to be banished out of sight. Some, sad to say, seem to lament the loss of the Mosaic era, when those guilty of moral failures found themselves "under a pile of stones."

Those who are known to have failed become the object of gossip, humiliation, unkindness, and retribution. We want them to "vanish and disappear" because we fear that their failure is contagious, and we or the cause we embrace might probably get infected by the effect of their "moral sins."

Spiritual failure can so destabilize and disorient its victim that every iota of knowledge can take flight from the gray matter in a matter of minutes. With a heart already grieved and hurting, harsh and cruel treatment suffered at the hands of "those who haven't fallen," can make the condition of the "sinner" even worse. And, as a consequence, those who suffer from the consequences of their self-inflicted wounds of sin are sitting ducks, just exposed for ultimate failure (death) to close in for the kill and terminate their lives (in suicide).

This has happened all too many times. Yet Failure is not tired yet. He's prowling about for more victims. Sadly, he will have his way with a lot of people still. I hope it will not be you or anyone within your sphere of influence: family, friends, neighbors, colleagues at work, church members, and others that you know.

But spiritual failure—and any kind of failure—doesn't have to be the end of a person. We can rise out of failure, and depending on how we handle it, we can transform our failures into successes. The book you hold in your hands, *Six More Chances*, is concrete evidence that something good can come out of failure!

> ANY TIME WE VIOLATE ANY OF THE
> PRECEPTS IN GOD'S MORAL LAW
> (THE TEN COMMANDMENTS OR DECALOGUE),
> WE HAVE EXPERIENCED A "MORAL FALL."

MY PERSONAL EXPERIENCE

You see, I also suffered a "moral failure." When I fell, a lot of people believed that I was fallen forever. As I'll later explain, I suffered reproach of friends and foes, misunderstanding, misrepresentation, slander, intrigue, derision, ostracism, betrayal, unkindness and the wish by some that I would forever be banished away by God and man.

I had flashes of doubtful moments when the future looked terribly gloomy, overshadowed by that singular past. I lost all joy in the present and was afraid of the future. I didn't know what to do most of the time, except pray and quietly reflect. Failure stared me in the face and gloried in his apparent success over me. I was crushed, thinking I would be his victim forever.

But God lovingly drew me out of Failure's clutches and set me on the path to success—to victory over those adversities and to usefulness in His hands. This is why I can truthfully say today in my native Ghanaian language, *"M'akoma Ahye Ma"* (My heart is full). Out of the joy of what God has done for me, I seek to speak to those who have similarly failed, or done something so terrible that they find forgiveness from man very wanting and that acceptance by God must be impossible.

You think you're finished and that all hope is lost? Take courage in the fact that God does not throw any repentant soul away. It does not matter if you're rejected by man on account of a failure considered too grievous to be forgiven. God is in the business of accepting His lost, prodigal children back home, no matter how filthy they are. Just find your way back home to where He's waiting, with arms ready to envelop you in love and clean you up. For you He died that you might live with Him forever. For you He waits, that He might brush off the dirt from your fall and set you back on track.

The goal of this final chapter of our book is simple: Regardless of your failure, God can help you handle failure well. He did it for me. He can do the same for you as well. *The key is rising up again after a failing*—rising up in the strength of the Lord because you have "six more chances" left. God gives us not just second chances, but "six more chances." Nay, "more than six more chances." This should be a cause for rejoicing. For me, I can only say "*M'akoma ahye ma!*" (My heart is full!)

SIX MORE CHANCES: KEEP GETTING UP!

John Maxwell says it best: "Failure is not fatal. Only failure to get back up is." Our attitude determines whether our failure will be a setback or a stepping-stone. From my personal experience I have discovered that *people can fail into success if they don't stay down after a fall*. "Failing into success" calls for a resilient attitude. We can only fail into success if we keep getting up after a fall.

There is a Japanese proverb that says, "Fall down seven times and get up eight." This maxim speaks to the concept of resilience and determination. No matter how many times you get knocked down, you must keep getting up again. This philosophy or ethic is ingrained in the Japanese culture to embrace business, education, sports, martial arts etc. The basic message is, "Don't give up. Keep rising up."

The Bible expresses a similar sentiment. In fact, it is stated in a several places (PROVERBS 24:16; PSALM 37:23-25; 2 CORINTHIANS 4:8, 9; MICAH 7:8, 9; AND OTHERS). However, it was King Solomon, the wisest man who ever lived, who said it best in one of his proverbs. I refer to it as the "Six More Chances" mindset towards failure.

We're accustomed to hearing that God is a God of second chances. But as we'll soon discover, He is a God of "six more chances." In fact, He is a God of "much more than six more chances."

SIX MORE CHANCES

A "six more chances" mindset towards failure enables us to fail forward. To fail into success. Here is how Solomon states it in Proverbs 24:16:

> "For a righteous man may fall seven times and rise again, but the wicked shall fall by calamity" (NKJV).

Another version states it thus:

> "The godly may trip seven times, but they will get up again. But one disaster is enough to overthrow the wicked" (NLT).

If a righteous man rises again after falling seven times, the implication, mathematically speaking, is that when he first fell he had "six more chances" left! In other words, whenever we fail—whenever we fall—we must tell ourselves: "This is only one out of seven chances. I have six more chances left."

Lest I be misunderstood, I'm not saying this passage gives us a license to keep falling. I'm simply saying, If you fall, don't despair. Get up. Your one fall is not the end of you. You have "six more chances."

Perhaps the best way to explain the "Six More Chances" mindset towards failure is to share with you part of a sermon presented to our students at The University of Michigan several years ago, when I was the Director of Public Campus Ministries. The speaker was David Asscherick, the Director of ARISE and currently also Co-Director of Light Bearers. He titled his sermon, "Keep Getting Up."

Over the years, I have shared his message with scores of students, all of whom have been positively impacted by it. In the months following the pain and shame of my moral fall, I have ruminated a good many times on this message. It has played a vital role in my spiritual healing and growth.

I agree with David that the idea of "keep getting up" is "the single secret to succeeding in the Christian walk." It is the same concept as my "Six

More Chances" principle of success through failure. In order not to take anything away from David's presentation, I'm reproducing it in its entirety, hoping that the reader can "hear" or feel the heart of one of my favorite speakers. Asscherick was a former punk rocker, professional skateboarder and rock climber, became a Christian at the age of 23, and is now Seventh-day Adventist minister.[2]

> SINNING IS NOT INEVITABLE FOR THE COMMITTED CHRISTIAN, BUT GETTING BACK UP MUST BE!

KEEP GETTING UP

Floyd Patterson, nicknamed the Gentleman of Boxing, was the youngest man to ever win the American Heavyweight Boxing Championship. In a recent interview with boxing historian, Bert Sugar, Patterson was reminded by Mr. Sugar that he had been knocked down more than any other boxer in history. The great boxer humbly replied, "Yes, but I got up more times than anyone."

He didn't win the championship by *not falling down*; he won the championship by getting up.

And so it is for the Christian. The single secret to succeeding in the Christian walk is to *keep getting up*. Solomon understood this point, and articulated it with typical accuracy in Proverbs 24:16, "For a just man falls seven times, and rises up again: but the wicked shall fall into mischief."

You will notice that both the righteous ("just") and the wicked fall. So the difference between the righteous and the wicked is not that the righteous doesn't fall, but that he gets up after he falls. But let's take this a step further, shall we?

According to this verse, who falls *more*? The answer is unavoidable, isn't it? It's the righteous man. The righteous man falls more precisely because he keeps getting up. It is axiomatic that you cannot fall down unless you were standing up. According to our verse, the wicked falls just once because when he falls he stays down. Unlike the righteous man, he doesn't get back up.

Judas Versus Peter

Imagine if we traced the lives of Peter and of Judas from the time of the betrayal of Jesus in Gethsemane to the respective end of each of their lives. Who, over the course of his life, from Gethsemane on, fell more? Judas fell by betraying Jesus for a pittance; and instead of getting up, he put an end to his life by a final fall from a tree, dangling horribly at the end of a noosed rope. Peter fell, too; he denied his Lord thrice, then lived for many more years during which he fell again and again. The reality of further failure is seen in Galatians 2, where Peter reverts back to his bigoted ways in his relations with the Gentiles. His reaction to failure is especially revealed in his later response to the one who publicly reproved him at that time, as he testifies to the inspiration of the writings of Paul, identifying them with "the rest of Scripture."[3]

Peter had a lifetime to make mistakes, to sin, to fall. And to keep getting up. Judas fell that once, and didn't get back up. So who fell more? Peter. Which will be saved? Peter.

So we repeat, with Solomon, "A righteous man falls seven times and rises up again: but the wicked shall fall into mischief."

That the righteous falls more (again, because he keeps getting up) than the wicked in no way condones or *excuses* sin. Rather, it puts sin (falling) in perspective. To *not fall* is better, far better, of course. (No bipedal creature would argue this point!) And what's more, in the power of God (and His power alone), not falling is a present possibility! Hear the words of Holy Scripture: "Now unto Him That is able to keep you from falling, and to present *you* faultless before the presence of His glory with exceeding joy, to the only wise God our Saviour, *be* glory and majesty, dominion and power, both now and ever. Amen" (JUDE 24, 25).

But the earlier point still stands: *If* (not *when*) you fall ... get back up. Because sinning is not inevitable for the committed Christian, but getting back up must be!

Proceed With the Process

Salvation is by grace alone, through faith alone. This is not in dispute for the committed Protestant Christian. Justification is instantaneous—the moment a sinner accepts the life, death, and resurrection of Jesus Christ as his only hope, he is *accounted as righteous*. In the inimitable words of Ellen White in *Steps to Christ*,

"If you give yourself to Him, and accept Him as your Saviour, then, sinful as your life may have been, for His sake you are accounted righteous. Christ's character stands in place of your character, and you are accepted before God just as if you had not sinned" (page 64).

No one would seriously deny that Paul of Tarsus was the consummate champion of the Good News (Gospel) of righteousness by faith. Paul's advocacy of the evangel of faith included the notion that salvation involves an ongoing *process*. The following excerpts are representative, being some of the best known and best loved Pauline passages:

For I am not ashamed of the Gospel of Christ: for it is the power of God unto salvation to everyone that believeth; to the Jew first, and also to the Greek. For therein is the righteousness of God revealed from faith to faith: as it is written, The just shall live by faith. (ROMANS 1:16, 17).

But we all, with open face beholding as in a glass the glory of the Lord, are changed into the same image from glory to glory, even as by the Spirit of the Lord. (2 CORINTHIANS 3:18).

For which cause we faint not; but though our outward man perish, yet the inward man is renewed day by day. (2 CORINTHIANS 4:16).

Notice the phrases: "from faith to faith," "from glory to glory," and "day by day." What grammatical and theological function do these phrases serve in each of these respective passages? The answer is incontrovertible. They each communicate a *process*.

For Paul, salvation involved a process. The dictionary defines process as "a series of actions or steps taken in order to achieve a particular end."

Salvation involves steps. Doesn't the name *Steps to Christ* make very good sense? Indeed, it does!

The Christian Walk Not the Christian Leap

I have never heard anyone refer to it as the Christian leap. But frequently and colloquially we refer to it as the Christian *walk*. Think of it: Just how far could even the most athletic among us leap? Fifteen feet (4.6 meters)? Twenty feet (6.1 meters)? The current world record for the long jump is held by American Mike Powell, who jumped 29.363 feet (8.95 meters) at the World Track and Field Championships in Tokyo, Japan, in 1991.

It is not easy to leap 29 feet (8.8 meters). But it is quite easy for the average person to walk that distance. In fact, great distances can be covered by walking. I just recently finished a marvelous book called *The Places in Between*, in which author Rory Stewart documents part of his 6,000-mile walk across Asia. It took him 21 months.

The life of the believer is frequently and rightly called the Christian *walk* because it is just that—a walk. "For we walk by faith, not by sight," said Paul in 2 Corinthians 5:7. Walking takes time, yes, but you can cover vast distances. So, too, with the walk of faith.

Instant Lemonade

There is such a thing as instant lemonade. And instant tea. And even instant coffee. But there is no such thing as *instant sanctification*. Sanctification is the Biblical, theological term for walking with God. It does happen—praise God for that—but it does not happen instantaneously. Not according to the Pauline passages cited above, and not according to Ellen White:

> There is no such thing as instantaneous sanctification. True sanctification is a daily work, continuing as long as life shall last. (*THE FAITH I LIVE BY*, P. 116.)

> Let us be growing Christians. We are not to stand still. We are to be in advance today of what we were yesterday; every day learning to be more trustful, more fully relying upon Jesus. Thus we are to grow up. You do not at one bound [leap] reach perfection; sanctification is the work of a lifetime. (*SELECTED MESSAGES*, BK. 3, P. 193.)

Sanctification is the progressive work of a lifetime. (IBID., P. 202.)

Not surprisingly for Seventh-day Adventists, Ellen White's view of the processes involved in salvation squares perfectly with the apostle Paul's.

Christianity does not take place in one fell swoop, one grand leap. Do yourself a favor and disabuse your mind of that un-Biblical notion. The Christian walk is just that, a walk. And walking great distances—like from unholiness to holiness [or, in our case here, from failure to success]—takes time.

And if you fall while walking, what to do? Simple: Get back up.

Availability of Forgiveness

I cannot tell you how many times I have failed—utterly let myself, my Lord, and my family down. It is too many to count—not that I'd want to even if I could. You know how it is: You've blown it. You said the wrong thing. Or you looked at that Web site that you swore you never would do again. Or you gossiped, after promising yourself you wouldn't do it again. Or you … (fill in the blank).

It can be difficult at such times to believe that forgiveness is still there, still waiting for us to ask for it, still ready to be bestowed by two nail-scarred hands. There have been many times when, with trembling hand, I've opened the Bible hoping that it was still there. I arrive at 1 John chapter 1, half expecting verse 9 to be gone. I'm just sure that it's going to skip right from verse 8 to verse 10....

But it's always there. Every time.

Every time.

And if it's there, then I can still claim it. And I do! And you should, too! The one time that verse won't be there for me is the time I don't go there to claim it, to read it, to believe it. Praise God for verse 9!

"If we confess our sins, He is faithful and just to forgive us our sins, and to cleanse us from all unrighteousness." 1 JOHN 1:9.

Read it. Believe it. Claim it. Live it.

And as if that weren't enough, chapter 2, verse 1 is always there to encourage me along:

"My little children, these things write I unto you, that ye sin not. And if any man sin, we have an Advocate with the Father, Jesus Christ the Righteous." 1 JOHN 2:1.

I hear John saying, "In the unlikely event that one of you sins, Jesus is there for you. He is your Advocate. He is your Helping Hand. He is your Saviour. He'll help you to get *back up again*." Remember, *not falling* is better—far better—than falling and then getting back up! On your own you could never do it, "but with God all things are possible" (MATTHEW 19:26).

And with God what is *possible* becomes *probable*. And what is *probable* becomes *certain*. "I can do all things through Christ Which strengtheneth me" (PHILIPPIANS 4:13). "For it is God Which worketh in you both to will and to do of *His* good pleasure" (2:13).

> WITH GOD WHAT IS POSSIBLE BECOMES PROBABLE. AND WHAT IS PROBABLE BECOMES CERTAIN.

Learning to Hate

God hates sin. I don't entirely, yet. But I want to. And God wants me to. Each time I get back up and confess my sin and turn to Jesus, I am giving God permission to do something miraculous in my life. I am giving Him permission to supernaturally, through the power of His indwelling Spirit, create in me a God-given repugnancy for sin.

I cannot manufacture a revulsion for sin. Naturally, every fiber and nerve in my body craves sin—the lust of the flesh, the lust of the eyes, and the pride of life. Only God can put enmity for sin inside of me. And every time I get up and look with disgust at the vomit I've just wallowed in, God is putting that enmity inside me by His Spirit. He's helping me, teaching me, to hate what He hates, to loathe what He loathes.

Because sin killed Jesus. Don't forget it. Sin isn't cute. It isn't funny. It isn't small. (And it isn't inevitable, either!)

Sin is the most deadly cancer in the universe. A cancer so powerful that it killed the Son of God when it was placed squarely on His shoulders amidst Gethsemane's olive groves. He limped painfully, barely making it to Calvary because of the terrible weight on His back. And it wasn't the *patibulum* (Latin for crossbar). It was sin. The weight of the sin of the world.

The Bible says that Jesus hated sin. "Thou hast loved righteousness, and hated iniquity; therefore God, even Thy God, hath anointed Thee with the oil of gladness above Thy fellows" (HEBREWS 1:9).

Part of getting up is asking God to give you power, grace, strength, and poise to not fall down again. To hate sin. To loathe the vomit of iniquity. To hate what God hates. To hate what pierced your Lord and King.

Because if you keep putting your faith in Jesus Christ, one of these times you're going to fall for that sin (you know which one) for the last time. You'll get up from it, and, in the power and grace of God, walk away from it. Forever.

From the Old to the New

In Luke 5, Jesus told a series of three parables in which He made the case for the danger and illogic of mingling the old and the new.

> "And He spake also a parable unto them; No man putteth a piece of a new garment upon an old; if otherwise, then both the new maketh a rent, and the piece that was taken out of the new agreeth not with the old. And no man putteth new wine into old bottles; else the new wine will burst the bottles, and be spilled, and the bottles shall perish. But new wine must be put into new bottles; and both are preserved. No man also having drunk old wine straightway desireth new: for he saith, The old is better." (LUKE 5:36–39).

Scholars are generally agreed that Jesus is here speaking of the transition from a pre-Messianic to a post-Messianic economy in the Judaism of His day. The scribes and Pharisees could not fit the new wine of Jesus' Messianic identity and teachings into the old wine of their narrow misinterpretation of the Jewish religion.

But there is also a very real sense in which Jesus is here speaking of the transition from old life to new life, old man to new man, in a personal, experiential sense. These parables are metaphors for the transition from old to new in the life of the believer.

Notice that Jesus is appealing to our common sense in each of the parables. He introduces each of them by saying, "No man" does such and such. The message is simple: Think about it; *no one* does this. Use your noggin, Jesus is saying.

Now look particularly at the last verse. Jesus uses the key word, "straightway." The NKJV translates this as "immediately."

A drunk can come to love Welch's Grape Juice, but it doesn't happen immediately. It takes *time*. It involves a *process*. (Sounds just like Paul and Ellen White!) The old wine represents the old life, the old ways, the old movies, the old Web sites, the old parties, the old drugs, the old sensuality, the old … (fill in the blank).

Jesus says that the man accustomed to the old alcoholic wine can grow to love the new and the fresh and loathe the old, but it takes time. It doesn't happen "immediately." But it does happen. It does.

I know. Because I am living it. And hopefully you are, too. Out with old (by God's grace), and in with new (also by God's grace).

Does Often *Mean* Often?

The book *Steps to Christ* [by E. G. White] has saved my spiritual life more than once. How can a book so small and so simple be so completely amazing? I don't know, but it is.

I make an effort to read this book at least once a year (sometimes it's closer to ten times in a given year!). It is just that powerful, and valuable. And simple.

Here is one of my favorite excerpts from this power-packed mini-volume:

There are those who have known the pardoning love of Christ and who really desire to be children of God, yet they realize that their character is imperfect, their life faulty, and they are ready to doubt whether their hearts have been renewed by the Holy Spirit. To such I would say, Do not draw back in despair. We shall often have to bow down and weep at the feet of Jesus because of our shortcomings and mistakes, but we are not to be discouraged. Even if we are overcome by the enemy, we are not cast off, not forsaken and rejected of God. No; Christ is at the right hand of God, Who also maketh intercession for us. Said the beloved John, "These things write I unto you, that ye sin not. And if any man sin, we have an Advocate with the Father, Jesus Christ the Righteous." (1 JOHN 2:1.—E. G. WHITE, *STEPS TO CHRIST*, P. 64.)

Read it again. And again, until these words pierce right into your heart. Believe them. They are true. And they are for you.

"Often."

"Do not draw back in despair."

"We are not to be discouraged."

"We are not cast off."

"[We are] not forsaken and rejected by God."

"No."

The message is clear. (Could it be any clearer?) Even if you fall and fail (especially when you fall and fail!), go to the cross—to the *Christ* of the cross. Bow down. Ask for forgiveness. Trust Jesus. Take His hand. Get up. Repeat as often as necessary. Keep getting up.

Just like Floyd.

> "NATIONS 'RISE AND FALL,'
> BUT THE SAINTS 'FALL AND RISE'!"

More Than Six More Chances

"Keep getting up." It means whenever you fail, whenever you fall into sin, don't be discouraged into quitting. Go to Christ for forgiveness. As often as you fail, go to Him. He will abundantly pardon. What better way to capture the "Six More Chances" mindset towards failure?

The one harmonious chorus throughout the Bible is "Don't stay down

when you fall. Keep getting up. For God is a God of 'six more chances.'"
Go to God for forgiveness and keep running the Christian race. The prophet
Micah says:

> "Do not rejoice over me, my enemy; *when I fall, I will arise* [I'll keep
> getting up]; when I sit in darkness, the LORD will be a light to me"
> (MICAH 7:8).

Notice that it is not "if I fall," but "when I fall." In the Christian walk,
we will sometimes (even often) fall. But when it happens, don't be discouraged. Rise after your fall—not in your might, but in the strength of Christ
alone. This is what I had in mind in one of my "thought nuggets" when I
wrote a piece titled:

> A MATTER OF SEQUENCE: "Nations 'rise and fall,' but the
> saints 'fall and rise'! All other human beings first 'live and die,' but Jesus
> 'died and lives.' It's all a matter of sequence. The fulcrum is He Who
> was born for the 'falling and rising of many.' "
> —*SKP* (*Meditations on Micah 7:8–10, 18, 19; Psalm 37:23, 24; Luke 2:34;
> Revelation 1:18*)

In fact, excepting Jesus, every single character of the Bible failed. What
set them apart as victors, and not failures, is that they didn't stay down.
Thus, we can say that hero and heroine of the Bible—understood the "six
more chances" principle.

⌒ SOLOMON—THE WISEST ONE:

> "For a righteous man may fall seven times and rise again,
> but the wicked shall fall by calamity" (PROVERBS 24:16, NKJV)

⌒ DAVID—THE GREAT SINGER:

> "The steps of a good man are ordered by the Lord, and He delights in
> his way. *Though he fall, he shall not be utterly cast down*; [implication: he rises
> after falling] for the Lord upholds him with His hand" (PSALM 37:23, 24).

JOB—THE GREAT SUFFERER:

"He shall deliver you in six troubles, yes, in seven no evil shall touch you" (JOB 5:19).

PETER—THE OVERCONFIDENT ONE:

Even Peter believed in the "six more chances" principle when he thought that we should forgive those who have wronged us seven times.

"Then Peter came to Him [Christ] and said, 'Lord, how often shall my brother sin against me, and I forgive him? Up to seven times?' " (MATTHEW 18:21).

If a wrongdoer, a person who has failed, should be forgiven seven times, the implication is that when the erring one fails once, he has six more chances!

JESUS—THE EXCEPTIONAL BUT MOST WOUNDED ONE OF ALL:

But here comes the surprise. Even Jesus taught the "six more chances" principle. Only for Him, it was *"much more* than six more chances."

To help you stay on this glorious track, let me repeat what I said earlier: If a righteous man rises again after falling seven times, the mathematical implication is that when he falls once, he has "six more chances" left! In other words, whenever we fail—whenever we fall—we must tell ourselves: "This is only one out of seven chances. I have six more chances left."

Now, when we reflect upon the response of Jesus to Peter's question above, it will become evident that our Lord's teaching on forgiveness implies that the sinner, the person who has failed, has "much more than six more chances."

"Then Peter came to Him and said, 'Lord, how often shall my brother sin against me, and I forgive him? Up to seven times?' Jesus said to him, 'I do not say to you, up to seven times, but up to seventy times seven' " (MATTHEW 18:21, 22).

Jesus said we should not forgive "seven times," that is we should not give people just "six more chances" after they fail once, but "seventy times seven" instances. At least 490 times. Which means if you fail, you have 489 more chances! "Much more than six more chances"! In other words, when you fail and are tempted to give up or not get up on your feet, tell yourself: I may be down, but I'm not out. I have at least 489 more chances left.

I say "at least" because Jesus does not count how many times we have sinned. The whole thrust of the parable in Matthew 18:21–35 is the unlimited pardon that is available to the sinner. He forgives those whose sins "are many" (LUKE 7:36–50).[4]

In algebraic terms, if "X" represents the "many" times you have fallen/sinned and received forgiveness, then after you fall once, you have "X–1" more chances. Now if X is uncountable, or is an infinite number, that innumerable amount of times less one results in equally infinite chances. This is why the Bible says,

"Many are the afflictions of the righteous, but the Lord delivers him out of them all" (PSALM 34:19).

I'll paraphrase it for our discussion that "many are the failures of God's people, but God forgives them all." This point is aptly conveyed by the apostle Paul.

PAUL—THE HONESTLY MISTAKEN ONE:

He understood the "much more than six more chances" attitude to failure when he referred to himself as the chief of sinners. No doubt, he was convinced that God's promises offer us "much more" than we can think or ask:

"Now to Him Who is able to do exceedingly abundantly above all that we ask or think, according to the power that works in us, to Him be glory in the church by Christ Jesus to all generations, forever and ever. Amen" (EPHESIANS 3:20, 21).

Let's reflect on what Paul is saying, noting the "much more-ness" of what God can do:

God is able.
God is able to do what *we ask*.

God is able to do what we ask or *think*.

God is able to do *all* that we ask or think.

God is able to do *above* all that we ask or think.

God is able to do *abundantly* above all that we ask or think.

God is able to do *exceedingly* abundantly above all that we ask or think.

How much more can Paul express the "much more-ness"? He's trying to capture for us the concept of unlimited possibilities. And as far as God's forgiveness is concerned it far exceeds all expectations.

A RECAP AND SOME IMPLICATIONS

So far, we've been trying to probe into the fact that we cannot out-sin God's forgiveness. No matter how low we have fallen, no matter how many times we have done so, there is always room for "one more" chance to get up. In fact, when you think you've messed up so badly again, just remember that "a righteous man falls seven times, but rises again." Your last messy situation is one less than seven of the chances.

Let me try summing up from some three or four key passages:

Proverbs 24:16

"For a righteous man may fall seven times and rise again, but the wicked shall fall by calamity."

At least two implications arise from this passage:

1. Both the righteous and the wicked fall. That's a given! No ifs, ands, or buts. It is a given fact. We should not be surprised that we experience loss or failure—business, health, spiritual, etc. With the wicked we fall into the same pit of failures. The only difference is that the righteous gets out of it. He gets up and keeps moving.

2. Though a righteous man falls seven times, he rises again, but the wicked are brought down by calamity" (PROVERBS 24:16). We may fall again and again, trouble may come again and again, we may struggle again and again … and again! But God has made adequate provision for us to rise—again and again and again. We shall keep getting up.

When a righteous man falls, his battered and bruised body still has the essential lifeblood in it and he does not thereby become a corpse. He is cleaned up and nursed back to health. The period of recuperation varies from person to person, but the righteous definitely need not remain fallen following failure.

The Psalmist David declares: "The Lord upholds all those who fall and lifts up all who are bowed down" (PSALM 145:14). God never intends that we stay down forever after we fall. He enables us to "rise up" and keep on walking with Him.

Psalm 37:23, 24

"The steps of a good man are ordered by the Lord, And He delights in his way. Though he fall, he shall not be utterly cast down; For the LORD upholds him with His hand."

1. The operative word is "though." "Though he fall." Some translations say, "When he falls." Note that it does not say, "If he falls." There is a big difference between "when" and "if." The latter states a probability; the former declares a certainty.

This is true in spiritual enterprise as well as in our practical, daily lives. An example from the practical realm is Job. Like him we also can:

~ go from wealthy to broke almost overnight.

~ witness the death of all our children overnight.

~ see our wives and husbands abandon us—marriage failure.

~ experience the cruel words and actions of folks who claim to be our friends, miserable comforters whose "help" is often worse than the arrows of our enemies.

And, yes, we will also fall spiritually. We may sometimes lose our way. Our Christian walk will at times falter. We may fall along the way. No one is exempt. The issue is not whether or not we fall, but it's what happens after we fall that makes all the difference. Though the righteous falls, "he shall not be utterly cast down."

2. When the Bible says, "The steps of a good man are *ordered* by the Lord," the word "ordered" implies that God knows ahead of time what will happen to His children and permits it to happen. He "orders" (he knows and permits) every step we take—the good and the bad. He knows ahead of time what will happen to you. Hence your fall doesn't catch God off guard. He knew Peter was going to fail (LUKE 22), but He permitted it and even told him ahead of time.

The verb "ordered" is very strong in the original Hebrew. It means to establish something so that it has a strong foundation. Proverbs 16:9 tells us that "in his heart a man plans his course, but the Lord determines his steps." It has the same basic meaning as Psalm 37:23.

Most of us know that God "directs" our steps (PROVERBS 3:6). But this verb ("ordered") is even stronger. God not only "directs" our steps, but He also "determines" or "orders" or "ordains" our steps. He knows and permits them. He is in control. God doesn't say, "Oops … I didn't see this coming upon My child! What am I going to do?"

> NOTHING EVER HAPPENS TO THE CHILD
> OF GOD BY LUCK, CHANCE, OR FATE.
> NO CIRCUMSTANCE—WHETHER GOOD
> OR BAD—CAN COME TO US APART
> FROM GOD'S KNOWLEDGE, PERMISSIVE WILL,
> AND PURPOSE FOR US.

No! There are no accidents with Him. Nothing ever happens to the child of God by luck, chance, or fate. No circumstance—whether good or bad—can come to us apart from God's knowledge, permissive will, and purpose for us. Or as E. G. White puts it:

In the annals of human history the growth of nations, the rise and fall of empires, appear as dependent on the will and prowess of man. The shaping of events seems, to a great degree, to be determined by his power, ambition, or caprice. But in the Word of God the curtain is drawn aside, and we behold, behind, above, and through all the play and counterplay of human interests and power and passions, the agencies of the all-merciful One, silently, patiently working out the counsels of His own will. (*EDUCATION*, P. 173.2)

God designs our trials so they will not destroy us.

This follows from all that I have stated earlier. Verse 24 assures us that though we may "stumble" or "fall" temporarily, we will not be utterly destroyed. God will not allow anything to permanently destroy our relationship with Him. Not even death itself can sever our strong connection with God. "He knows the way that I take; when He has tested me, I will come forth as gold" (JOB 23:10).

When we are "in the furnace" it is hard to believe that any good could result from the fiery trial. But God says, when it's all over we shall see "pure gold." We must believe this by faith, especially during difficult days when we have failed. God can reverse our misfortunes. The God of Joseph and Job is also our God during our moments of failure. Just as Joseph emerged from prison to palace, and just as Job received back everything he once lost, God can also ensure that we are "not utterly cast down."

Consider what Jesus said to Peter in the upper room on the night before He was crucified: "Simon, Simon, Satan has asked to sift you as wheat. But I have prayed for you, Simon, that your faith may not fail. And when you have turned back, strengthen your brothers" (LUKE 22:31, 32).

This statement deserves special notice because Jesus said it before Peter's threefold denial. In fact, Jesus said it just before Peter made his boastful promise of unending faithfulness. The point is, *Jesus saw it all coming, knew everything before it took place, and yet permitted it.* Christ knew of:

the boasting,
the teenage girl around the fire,
the swearing,
the repeated denials,

the shame,
the bitter tears,
the guilt,
the restoration.

From the Luke 22:31, 32 passage I gather the following profound insights about the Biblical view of spiritual failure:

1. Spiritual failure is part of the ongoing cosmic conflict or "great controversy" between Christ and Satan, wherein God wants to save us but Satan wants to destroy us. The battle in every spiritual failure is, ultimately, a battle between Satan and God Himself.

2. God foresees spiritual failure of His children coming but *permits* it; no spiritual failure catches God off guard—whether it is the failure of Peter, Abraham, David, Samson, Hezekiah, Isaiah, or any other of God's "classic eagles" (the heroes and heroines of the Bible).

3. The reason God *permits* (not causes) spiritual failure is to save us, not to destroy us. We know He wants to save us, hence Jesus "prays" for us. Satan is the one who wants to destroy us: to "sift us like wheat."

4. When God eventually saves us, He also restores us to His service: "And when you have turned back, strengthen your brothers"; God gives every forgiven and restored sinner an assignment. Notice that it is not "if you turn back," but "when you turn back"—and when you turn back, do something for God. (We know from the Book of Acts that Peter subsequently played a major role in the apostolic church, even writing two letters for our edification.)

5. The person who experiences forgiveness and restoration from spiritual failure has an obligation to help others: "Strengthen your brothers." In other words, a missionary spirit is always the fruit of repentance and the experience of forgiveness. (In the words of E. G. White, "The spirit of Christ is a missionary spirit. *The very first impulse of the renewed heart is to bring others also to the Saviour.*" (SEE *THE GREAT CONTROVERSY*, P. 70.2.)

Peter's failure is, perhaps, of the worst type. Unlike, say, the failure of Moses that displayed rashness, Peter's was *premeditated*, for our Lord had warned him that it would happen. Peter had no excuse. Moreover, *Peter's denial of Christ was deliberate* (lying is a deliberate act); *worse yet, a repetitious error* (*for he denied Christ three* times; talk about a repeat offender!). But here is the good news about the God Who gives us "six more chances":

If God can forgive this kind of spiritual failure—if God can somehow manage to use the failures of *willful*, repetitious sinners like Peter, Abraham, Samson, etc., to strengthen our faith and deepen our commitment—then He can surely use the other less dramatic kinds of failure which are common to our experience as well.

Oh, there's so much more that can be said about how Luke 22:31, 32 sheds greater light on the Psalm 37:23, 24 passage; how "the steps of a good man are *ordered* by the Lord.... *Though* he fall, he shall not be utterly cast down; for the Lord upholds him with His hand."

> THE PERSON WHO EXPERIENCES FORGIVENESS AND RESTORATION FROM SPIRITUAL FAILURE HAS AN OBLIGATION TO HELP OTHERS: "THE VERY FIRST IMPULSE OF THE RENEWED HEART IS TO BRING OTHERS ALSO TO THE SAVIOUR."

For now, it is important to emphasize that no spiritual failure catches God off guard. He permits it for our good and also for the good or the "strengthening" of others. This is why He upholds the believer with His hand. This is why the believer is not utterly cast down during his or her fall. This is another implication of the "six more chances" principle.

2 Corinthians 4:8, 9

"We are hard-pressed on every side, yet not crushed; we are perplexed, but not in despair; persecuted, but not forsaken; struck down, but not destroyed" (NKJV).

"We may be knocked down but we are never knocked out" (PHILLIPS).

"We get knocked down, but we get up again and keep going" (THE LIVING BIBLE).

Paul was knocked to the ground many times, but he was never permanently grounded. Through all the trials, struggles, and failures God always through Christ gave him the strength to get up and get back in the race. *He was knocked down, but he wasn't knocked out.*

Notice the contrast between Paul's *outward* circumstances and his *inward* comfort:

Outwardly "troubled on every side" but inwardly "not distressed."
Outwardly "perplexed" but inwardly "not in despair."
Outwardly "persecuted" but inwardly "not forsaken."
Outwardly "cast down" but inwardly "not destroyed."

What the apostle Paul describes in the above passage, he himself actually experienced. A few chapters later, he describes his experience thus (IN 2 CORINTHIANS 11:23–28):

Are they servants of Christ? I know I sound like a madman, but I have served Him far more! I have worked harder, been put in prison more often, been whipped times without number, and faced death again and again. Five different times the Jewish leaders gave me thirty-nine lashes. Three times I was beaten with rods. Once I was stoned. Three times I was shipwrecked. Once I spent a whole night and a day adrift at sea. I have traveled on many long journeys. I have faced danger from rivers and from robbers. I have faced danger from my own people, the Jews, as well as from the Gentiles. I have faced danger in the cities, in the deserts, and on the seas. And I have faced danger from men who claim to be believers but are not. I have worked hard and long, enduring many sleepless nights. I have been hungry and thirsty and have often gone without food. I have shivered in the cold, without enough clothing to keep me warm.

> YOU MAY BE AT THE END OF YOUR ROPE,
> BUT YOU ARE NOT AT THE END
> OF YOUR HOPE.

Then, besides all this, I have the daily burden of my concern for all the churches. (NLT)

Paul was knocked down several times, but he wasn't knocked out. As with Paul, so with us. When faced with defeat, we too can have the inner strength, through Christ, to turn failure into victory. No matter what we've gone through or are currently going through: defeat, mistakes, missteps, scandal, etc.

Someone has said, "You may be at the end of your ROPE, but you are not at the end of your HOPE. You may be down in the deep ditches of defeat and despair, but you need not stay there. Through Christ you can get up again and go on."

"Man's extremity is God's opportunity." God is always at His best when we are at our worst. God can at all times; we are helpless and *can't*. God is always at work, even when we are at rock bottom! Let's look at the evidence:

Adam was down, but God lifted him.
Jacob was down, but God lifted him.
Joseph was down, but God lifted him.
Moses was down, but God lifted him.
Miriam was down, but God lifted her.

Aaron was down, but God lifted him.
David was down, but God lifted him.
Samson was down, but God lifted him.
Elijah was down, but God lifted him.
Hezekiah was down, but God lifted him.
Mary Magdalene was down, but God lifted her.
Peter was down, but God lifted him.

The whole history of humanity testifies to the truth of Paul's statement: *"We are hard-pressed on every side, yet not crushed; we are perplexed, but not in despair; persecuted, but not forsaken; struck down, but not destroyed"* (2 CORINTHIANS 4:8, 9, NKJV). Or as another translation has it, "We may be knocked down but we are never knocked out" (PHILLIPS). "We get knocked down, but we get up again and keep going" (THE LIVING BIBLE).

> FAILURE IS NOT DETERMINED BY
> THE NUMBER OF MISTAKES WE MAKE IN LIFE;
> IT IS HOW WE RESPOND TO THEM.
> BEING KNOCKED DOWN DOESN'T MEAN WE'RE
> KNOCKED OUT. LIKE THE DONKEY IN THE WELL,
> WHEN WE FACE ADVERSITY, WE SHOULD
> "SHAKE IT OFF AND STEP UP!"

God knows how to lift us up out of our predicaments. He knows how to fix our broken worlds: broken hearts, broken hopes, broken homes, and broken health. There is not a problem that Christ cannot fix. He brings beauty out of ugly situations. New growth out of ash heaps. Sweet-smelling life out of foul-smelling rottenness.

The above facts testify to a God Who gives people "six more chances" after they fall. They speak to us to keep getting up.

What Do All These Things Mean?

1. You're not a failure because you fall … only if you don't get back up. If you get up just once more than you fall, then you're a success! That's called "failing forward." Or failing into success.

2. One reason why we stay down when we have fallen is the feeling that our mistakes or sins are irredeemable. But this should not be so. Failure is not determined by the number of mistakes we make in life; it is how we respond to them. Being knocked down doesn't mean we're knocked out. The fact that we're down doesn't mean we must stay down. Like the donkey's story we shared in chapter one, when we face adversity, we should *shake it off and step up!*

3. *Union with Christ is key.* The "wicked" fail because they're not in connection with Christ. But when the Christian is in union with Christ and kept by His divine power, he shall and does rise again sooner or later. Not by his own power and strength, but by the strength of the Lord. The believer rises by renewed repentance and faith in Christ, having received God's pardoning grace and mercy to heal his backslidings. "But the wicked shall fall into mischief" (PROVERBS 24:16).

The Biblical *teaching* about "six more chances" (the mindset that we should keep getting up and never quit) is applicable to every aspect of life: academic, professional, marital, spiritual … And both secular and sacred history confirm that those who did not stay down got up and became successful.

Contemporary Individuals Who Didn't Give Up

Not convinced? I again invite you to consider the following examples. These individuals became famous as a result of their amazing achievements. However, as is often the case, their success was not immediate, and they fell on their faces before they achieved their dreams.

Consider these facts:

~ During its first year, Coca-Cola only sold 400 bottles of Coke.

~ NBA basketballer Michael Jordan was cut from his high school basketball team.

~ The legendary children's book author Dr. Seuss was rejected by 23 publishers before the 24th took on his books.

Even Elvis Presley was banished from the Grand Ole Opry after one performance and told: "You ain't goin' nowhere, son." Oprah Winfrey was also fired from her television reporter's job and advised: "You're not fit for TV." All these individuals bounced back. Michael Jordan sums it up:

> I've missed more than 9,000 shots in my career. I've lost almost 300 games. Twenty-six (26) times, I've been trusted to take the game-winning shot and missed. I've failed over and over and over again in my life. And that is why I succeed.
>
> —*Michael Jordan*

This is the statement of a person who was initially disqualified from his high school basketball team. Instead of giving up, he honed his skills and developed an undying passion for the game. He later led the University of North Carolina Tar Heels to an NCAA championship as an underclassman and ultimately became the standard by which all NBA players after him are judged.

You want other examples? Consider these:

~ HENRY FORD had two failed businesses before he became a pioneer in the automotive industry. Perhaps referring to his earlier not-so-successful ventures, Ford once famously said, "Failure is the opportunity to begin again more intelligently."

~ STEVEN SPIELBERG dreamed of becoming a filmmaker early in life, but he hit a major roadblock when the University of Southern California film school rejected him not once, not twice, but three times. Undaunted, Spielberg blazed his own trail, becoming one of the most successful and respected movie directors in history.

Everyone can't succeed at everything, but taking some cues from these famous icons lends credence to the idea that learning from your mistakes and following your passions can often turn failure into opportunity.

Let me add one more example: *Steve Jobs*. We mentioned him in the first chapter of this *Six More Chances*. When Jobs died, his half-sister Mona Simpson rendered a eulogy for her half-brother. This is what she said about Steve Jobs:

> He was never embarrassed about working hard, even if the results were failures. If someone as smart as Steve wasn't ashamed to admit trying, maybe I didn't have to be.

From "The Power of Taking the Big Chance," a compendium of lessons Steve Jobs' colleagues learned from him, as reported by Steve Lohr in The *New York Times*:

> Mr. Jobs was also decisive in recognizing mistakes, even when they were his own. For example, he favored one model of a disk drive—for reading computer programs stored on small, removable so-called floppy disks—while other members of the team championed another design. They kept their disk project going surreptitiously. When they showed him the result, he embraced it. "He turned on a dime," Mr. Capps says. "Don't dwell on your mistakes. It's a great lesson."

QUOTES ON FAILURE

Let me call attention to some important quotes on never giving up when we fail:

"Failure is the cloud that temporarily hides the sun.
It is not the death or obliteration of the sun."
—*SKP*

"What ought to be important, as far as failure is concerned,
is what you do about your failure."
—*SKP*

"Failure is inevitable when we embark upon innovation and change."
—*SKP*

"Failure is an expensive tuition in the school of success."
—*SKP*

"Failure is the mother of success."
—*Chinese Proverb*

"Failures are really mini successes.
—*Rob Diana*

"Failure is just evidence that you haven't mastered the task yet."
—*Amy Edmondson*

"Failure is success if we learn from it."
—*Malcolm S. Forbes*

"Success tastes much sweeter when we know what failure tasted like. We appreciate success better when we have known failure before."
—*Unknown*

"An inventor fails 999 times, and if he succeeds once, he's in. He treats his failures simply as practice shots."
—*Charles F. Kettering*

"Failure should be our teacher, not our undertaker. Failure is delay, not defeat. It is a temporary detour, not a dead end. Failure is something we can avoid only by saying nothing, doing nothing, and being nothing."
—*Denis Waitley*

"Keep on beginning and failing. Each time you fail, start all over again, and you will grow stronger until you have accomplished a purpose—not the one you began with perhaps, but one you'll be glad to remember."
—*Anne Sullivan*

"Failures are finger posts on the road to achievement."
—*C. S. Lewis*

"Remember the two benefits of failure. First, if you do fail, you learn what doesn't work; and second, the failure gives you the opportunity to try a new approach."
—*Roger von Oech*

"It is not the critic who counts, not the man who points out how the strong man stumbled, or where the doer of deeds could have done better. The credit belongs to the man who is actually in the arena, whose face is marred by dust and sweat *and blood*, who strives valiantly, who errs and comes short again and again, who knows the great enthusiasms, the great devotions, and spends himself in a worthy cause, who at best knows achievement and who at the worst if he fails at least fails while daring greatly so that his place shall never be with those cold and timid souls who know neither victory nor defeat."
—*Theodore Roosevelt*

"It is on our failures that we base a new and different and better success."
—*Havelock Ellis*

"Never confuse a single defeat with a final defeat."
—*F. Scott Fitzgerald*

DON'T QUIT

The implication of "six more chances" is that we must never quit. We must keep getting up.

"Defeat doesn't finish a man—quit[ting] does. A man is not finished when he's defeated. He's finished when he quits."
—*Richard M. Nixon*

In other words, if we don't quit, we won't fail. One preacher's summary:

1. YOUR STRUGGLES ARE NECESSARY—**FIGHT ON!**

2. YOUR FATHER HAS NOT FORGOTTEN YOU—**HANG ON!**

3. YOUR FUTURE IS ASSURED—**WALK ON!**

Fight on! Hang on! Walk on!

BIBLE CHARACTERS WHO DIDN'T QUIT

In the life of most any leaders you can think of, there is usually an occasion when it looked like it was over and they were greatly tempted to give up.

~ Moses fled from Egypt thinking his life was over, but really it had just begun. He was willing to try again, and God sent him back to deliver His people from Pharaoh.

~ David was not willing to quit even in the face of a giant named Goliath; and look what happened.

~ Elijah once prayed to die. But after God refreshed him, he got up and went and found his successor and anointed another king.

~ Peter thought it was over after he denied Christ. But he was willing to get up and go again, and God used him to preach the first sermon at Pentecost.

~ Jesus did not stop till He said, "It is finished!"

You can keep getting up and going again, too!

> AFTER FAILURE EMPTIES YOUR CUP, GOD'S GRACE CAN FILL THE CUP TO ITS BRIM AGAIN.

One Big Failure

Did you know that there was a man who kept trying when others would have quit? Had he given up, the United States of America would be a much different place today. Listen to his personal history:

Failed in business, age 22
Ran for Legislature–defeated, age 23
Again failed in business, age 24
Elected to Legislature, age 25
Sweetheart died, age 26
Had a nervous breakdown, age 27
Defeated for Speaker, age 29
Defeated for Elector, age 31
Defeated for Congress, age 34
Elected to Congress, age 37
Defeated for Congress, age 39
Defeated for Senate, age 46
Defeated for Vice President, age 47
Defeated for Senate, age 49
Elected President of the United States, age 51

That's the record of Abraham Lincoln. What would the U.S.A. look like today if Abraham Lincoln had given up early on? He stepped onto the stage of history by getting up and going again.

If you're discouraged, I encourage you: "Don't give up!"

THIS AUTHOR CHOSE NOT TO QUIT

We've spoken about contemporary individuals and Bible characters who chose not to quit. No doubt they were all armed by the "six more chances" mindset. But they're not alone. The author of this book, *Six More Chances*, also chose not to quit.

As I mentioned to you earlier, when I fell, a lot of people believed that I was fallen forever. I suffered reproach of friends and foes, misunderstanding, misrepresentation, slander, intrigue, derision, ostracism, betrayal, unkindness, and the wish by some that I would forever be banished away by God and man. There were several contrary voices that sought to convince me that the sun had set for me and there was no hope for me to be useful to the Lord and indeed, to man, in any future way.

But I simply chose not to quit, armed as I was with the Word of God and faith in His ability to forgive, transform, and restore the sinner. I decided to keep going on. And the book you hold in your hands, *Six More Chances*, is concrete evidence that something good can come out of failure!

This book is strong proof that after Failure empties your cup, God's grace can fill the cup to its brim again. The Lord showed me that though the cloud might cover my sun for a while, it was by no means sunset for me. That I might have failed, but He was by no means done with me. That if I chose to get up from my fall, He would keep me moving, and I would not remain down and fallen. I chose not to stay down. I chose not to quit.

Those who fail and stay down, still remain in the pit where they fell. Time does not stand still. The old year of my failure has transitioned to a new one and paved the way for new things in my life. I sing now in the light, the songs I learned in the dark. I chose to keep moving, and today you hold in your hands a part of my story and the lessons learned from failure.

That you may understand why my heart is full of gratitude, let me share with you the announcement I made to the world on New Year's Day, the day I completed the manuscript *of Six More Chances*.

"M'AKOMA AHYE MA"
MY NEW YEAR'S DAY MESSAGE

"M'akoma Ahye Ma" in one of our native Ghanaian languages means, "My Heart Is Full." I find this to be my experience as I look back on last year and look forward to this New Year.

Last year was a painful one for me personally. I suffered a deep pain far worse than death, as a result of sin. The year started for me with renewed commitment to God and His work at secular universities around the world. I made that commitment at the end of the 2010 GYC meeting in Baltimore, Maryland.

GYC stands for Generation of Youth for Christ. This Bible-based grass-roots youth movement was birthed through our ministry to public university students. The attendance at the GYC meeting peaked to over 6,000.

The theme at that event was "No Turning Back," and I presented a series of messages on "Radical Commitment."

From this spiritually uplifting 2010 GYC event, I proceeded to a mission assignment on a secular university campus overseas. Sad to say, at the end of a very fruitful spiritual endeavor, on the very last day of my ministry assignment, I experienced a moral fall: adultery. I had taught integrity while on the mountaintop of faithfulness. What would I now do, now that I lay in the valley of unfaithfulness?

> RADICAL COMMITMENT MEANS GOING ALL THE WAY IN DOING RIGHT. OR AS AN AFRICAN PROVERB SAYS, "IF YOU'RE GOING TO BE BALD ON YOUR HEAD, YOUR BALDNESS MUST AS WELL EXTEND TO YOUR NECK."

The Holy Spirit reminded and convicted me of the messages at the 2010 GYC meeting. Radical commitment means going all the way in doing right. Or as an African proverb says, *"If you're going to be bald on your head, your baldness must as well extend to your neck."* Thus, I made a choice to take full responsibility for my sin, however costly it might be. And costly it was.

As a consequence of my spiritual failure, I resigned from my employment with the Michigan Conference, and from my role as Director of CAMPUS, the umbrella organization for our ministry to public university students in Michigan (CAMPUS is the birthplace, headquarters, and sponsor of GYC). As a further consequence, I also surrendered my ministerial credential, resigned from the GYC board, and submitted myself to discipline by my local church.

The outlook was bleak at many different levels. However, in divine love, the Lord helped me up, brushed the dirt off me, and has been leading me on an upward journey not previously traversed in my relationship with Him.

While I regret the circumstances of my spiritual failure, I am overwhelmed at the goodness of the Lord in using my fall to teach me new truths, reaffirm promises not fully grasped, use me as a channel to reach out to many wounded eagles who, like me, on account of their own self-inflicted wounds, felt burdened by the load of guilt. It was a productive and rewarding year, in spite of the pain, shame, and pause in my public ministry. Looking back, I enthusiastically say *"M'akoma Ahye Ma"* (My heart is full)!

Last year was thus a year of lessons, learned painfully and quietly in the dark. In my resignation letter, I wrote that I was taking time off from center stage to recharge my spiritual batteries. That part of the letter reads:

"As for my future plans, I intend to spend some time with my family, do some prayerful reflection and study, and help in the orderly and smooth transition of the new CAMPUS leadership to be appointed by the Michigan Conference. Consequently, all speaking appointments are being canceled. Although my passion for youth training and empowerment has not waned, the rest of my life is in God's hands."

I have learned so many songs in the dark that I could not have learned while in the full glare of the sun. (I have shared a few of these "Songs in the Dark" with my Facebook friends and others in the form of weekly "thought nuggets.") I have experienced the love of God, that had always been there for me but which I never fully realized, in ways that I couldn't have experienced otherwise.

On one hand, I have suffered misunderstanding by friends—even ostracism and betrayal in one or two cases, and misrepresentation, slander, intrigue, and derision by those who oppose the principles I stand for, and the wish by some that I would forever be banished away by God and man. On the other hand, I have gained new friendships, learned new truths, and been called to minister in my personal capacity in ways that were not possible before.

As I look back at that painful period when the future seemed bleak and unsure and compare that with now, I am awed by the Lord's goodness in taking repentant ones back to the full joy of sonship with Him. Every fiber of my being pulsates with the emboldening knowledge that I am not a castaway. And my heart bursts out in full praise, *"M'akoma Ahye Ma."*

To all those who reached out to me and my family during that difficult time, we offer our sincere and deep appreciation for your spiritual, social, financial, and every other form of support. And we even want to thank those whose comments were cruel, to whom we are also indebted. For the Lord found fit use for all forms of response to teach us valuable lessons. For the comments and gestures from friends and foes, we can honestly say, *"M'akoma Ahye Ma."*

Indeed, strange as it may seem, among the most profitable blessings have been the pain resulting from the consequences of my sin. Though it was painful and shameful to have owned up to my sin publicly, by the grace of God, I am learning that pain is not merely the price of sin, but investment in righteousness. For it is in facing the painful results of sin that God prepares us for the rich blessings of His righteousness.

> SOMEONE CAN LITERALLY STEP OUT OF TIME, JOURNEY TO OUR BYGONE YEARS, AND FIX YESTERDAY'S BROKEN HOPES. JESUS CHRIST IS THE SAME YESTERDAY, TODAY, AND FOREVER. HE ALONE CAN GIVE US A BRAND-NEW YESTERDAY.

The New Year is here. I cheerfully look forward to seeing how the Lord may use me this year. Going by the way He's come through in the past, I know I have no need to fear, for God has given me *a brand-new yesterday*. He has given me a secure foundation to build my house of faith today. As I explained in one of my weekly "Songs in the Dark" thought nuggets,

"Yesterday is the foundation upon which we build houses of today and tomorrow. Though we're able to reside in the homes of today's challenges and in those of tomorrow's unknowns, often we're unable to live with yesterday's regrets. Yesterday represents spilled-milk experiences—lost opportunities, costly mistakes, shipwrecked relationships, lost innocence, and ineffaceable records. But Someone can literally step out of time, journey to our bygone years, and fix yesterday's broken hopes. Jesus Christ is the same YESTERDAY, today, and forever. He alone can give us a brand-new yesterday to enable us build our mansions."

—SKP (*A meditation on Hebrews 13:8; 2 Corinthians 5:1*)

"*M'akoma Ahye Ma*" (My heart is full) that God has given me a brand-new yesterday! As a tribute to Him for bestowing upon me His forgiving, transforming, and restorative grace, I want to offer this book, *Six More Chances*, as a small gift to the world.

But I capture the "much more than one more chance" with a Ghanaian phrase "*Ampa Ara M'akoma Ahye Ma.*"

"AMPA ARA, M'AKOMA AHYE MA"

"*Ampa Ara,*" in the Ghanaian language means, "truly," "indeed." Or "verily." Thus, "*Ampa Ara M'akoma Ahye Ma.*" literally means, Truly my heart is overwhelmed with joy. More literally, "My heart is full beyond its brim."

As I stated at the beginning of this chapter, when I fell, a lot of people believed that I was fallen forever. I had flashes of doubtful moments when the future looked very gloomy, overshadowed by that singular past. I lost joy in the present, and was afraid of the future. I didn't know what to do most of the time, except pray and quietly reflect. Failure stared me in the face and gloried in his apparent success over me. I was crushed and thought I would be his victim forever. But God lovingly drew me out of Failure's clutches and set me on the path to success.

It's the beginning of a new calendar year, as I conclude the draft of *Six More Chances*. It's also the start of a new life for me, a life that has come forth from the ashes of my failure, spoken into existence by the Creator of life Himself. A year ago I would have dreaded failing. Now I look back with gratitude on the path that has led me from my failure to the success that God measures out in appropriate doses for me now. The path is well worn with my tears and scars, but lasting are the lessons learned from it, and I am not complaining.

I don't know what you are going through as you're reading this book. I know what I went through. I failed, and the Lord cleaned me up. I can tell you heartily that the Lord can clean you up, too. Today is the first day of a New Year; so put your failure behind you, believing that it is possible to fail well into success. Get up in arms and do not succumb to the crushing weight of failure over your life. If there's anyone that can help you handle failure well, God can. He did for me. He can do the same for you as well. I went through much of last year with deep pain. It's been a long, arduous journey having to deal with the pain of my failure. Today I am no longer where I used to be in terms of that pain. *Six More Chances* is my incontrovertible evidence that true success is possible, in spite of having failed. It can be yours as well. The key is rising up again after a failing.

> DO NOT SUCCUMB TO THE CRUSHING
> WEIGHT OF FAILURE OVER YOUR LIFE.
> IF THERE'S ANYONE THAT CAN HELP YOU
> HANDLE FAILURE WELL, GOD CAN.

Failure doesn't have to be a dead end; it can be a valuable detour to aid us in life's journey. Setbacks need not set us back; they can be stepping-stones on which we can step upward and forward. Or as one student attendee of GYC stated in an e-mail to me, "Failure is what a man sees. God sees our failure as a stepping-stone and uses it as a foundation for a greater success. [Last year] may have been filled with what we call 'failures.' However, I know that God will continue to do great things, if not greater, through you and your ministry."

This book, *Six More Chances*, is not only my New Year's gift to young people and to the world, but also an announcement that "Yesterday" is behind me. It's a new day "Today." As explained in one of my "Songs in the Dark" thought nuggets,

"Today is the last day of yesterday and the first day of tomorrow. It's the conclusion to yesterday's chapter and the introduction to your new book. Why dwell on a written past, when you can write the future today?"
—*SKP (A meditation on Isaiah 43:18)*

On this first day of a New Year, and by means of the book *Six More Chances* I am announcing to the world that my "Yesterday" is behind me. My mind is made up "Today." And as far as the future is concerned, *"Ampa Ara M'akoma Ahye Ma."* (My heart is full beyond its brim) because with Jesus, tomorrow is as certain as the past:

"It's said: 'Yesterday is history, today is reality, and tomorrow a mystery.' Despite the mystery and unpredictability about the future, with God tomorrow is as certain as yesterday. Six months before Jesus' birth, His future mission was stated in the past tense: "God has VISITED and REDEEMED his people" (LUKE 1:68, 69). He was in the womb, and His earthly ministry, death, and resurrection lay in the future. Yet, Christ's mission is written in the past tense! With God, the future is already history. He's already set things in motion to accomplish our hopes for tomorrow. We can confidently face the future because Jesus Christ has visited our tomorrow and has made it as irreversibly certain as yesterday."
—*SKP (A meditation on Isaiah 44:6-8; 46:9, 10; Luke 1:67-80; Hebrews 13:8)*

It was faith that led me to take ownership of my sin and publicly confess it. It was an act of faith when I accepted the consequences of the sin—the pain, shame, and hurt—when I willingly resigned from my employment, surrendered my ministerial credentials, and submitted to church discipline. And it was an act of faith alone when I wrote in my resignation letter that "the rest of my life is in God's hands."

Sitting in the dark has confirmed to me that, in spite of the pain, humiliation, and hurt, the costly decision to do the right thing is always the right thing to do. For, secured in the hands of God my tomorrow—the rest of my life—is as sure as the past. Yes, indeed, because Jesus Christ has visited tomorrow and made it as irreversibly certain as yesterday, I can confidently face the future. The above "song in the dark" is another reason why I can say, *"Ampa Ara M'akoma Ahye Ma."* (My heart is full beyond its brim).

Because of the forgiving and restorative grace of God, the wounded eagle has been healed from its self-inflicted injuries and is ready to join all God's eagles in soaring again. From this day forward, I will sing to the world my many "songs in the dark."

To join me in singing those songs, dear reader, you also would need to take courage when you have to sit in the darkness of your failure. If you allow the Lord, your fall will not be fatal. There may be dark clouds, but your sun will not set.

Your wounds may have been very painful, but God's forgiving and restorative grace can enable you to soar again. In His Providence, He is molding you for a future task. Gather courage from the examples of the Bible characters of old. Their failure and rise again confirms the saying that "every saint has a *past* and every sinner has a *future!*"

If you have failed, don't give up. Don't stay down. Keep getting up. Remember, you have "six more chances." Nay, you have "much more than six more chances." This is reason enough for you to say, *"Ampa Ara M'akoma Ahye Ma."* (My heart is full beyond its brim).

> WITH GOD, THE FUTURE IS ALREADY HISTORY. WE CAN CONFIDENTLY FACE THE FUTURE BECAUSE JESUS CHRIST HAS VISITED OUR TOMORROW AND HAS MADE IT AS IRREVERSIBLY CERTAIN AS YESTERDAY.

"Let nothing hinder you. Fate has not woven its meshes about any human being so firmly that he need remain helpless and in uncertainty. Opposing circumstances should create a firm determination to overcome them. The breaking down of one barrier will give greater ability and courage to go forward. Press with determination in the right direction, and *circumstances will be your helpers, not your hindrances.*"[5]

"There are those who have known the pardoning love of Christ and who really desire to be children of God, yet they realize that their character is imperfect, their life faulty, and they are ready to doubt whether their hearts have been renewed by the Holy Spirit. To such I would say, Do not draw back in despair. We shall often have to bow down and weep at the feet of Jesus because of our shortcomings and mistakes, but we are not to be discouraged. Even if we are overcome by the enemy, we are not cast off, not forsaken and rejected of God. No; Christ is at the right hand of God, Who also maketh intercession for us. Said the beloved John, 'These things write I unto you, that ye sin not. And if any man sin, we have an Advocate with the Father, Jesus Christ the Righteous.' 1 John 2:1. And do not forget the words of Christ, 'The Father Himself loveth you.' (JOHN 16:27). He desires to restore you to Himself, to see His own purity and holiness reflected in you. And if you will but yield yourself to Him, He That hath begun a good work in you will carry it forward to the day of Jesus Christ. Pray more fervently; believe more fully. As we come to distrust our own power, let us trust the power of our Redeemer, and we shall praise Him Who is the health of our countenance.[6]

> IF YOU HAVE FAILED, DON'T GIVE UP.
> DON'T STAY DOWN. KEEP GETTING UP.
> REMEMBER, YOU HAVE "SIX MORE CHANCES."

NOTE:

The title "M'akoma Ahye Ma" ("My Heart Is Full") is also the title of a splendid musical composition that was written for me by a leading composer when he heard of my resignation. A brief history behind this song, the Scriptural themes employed, and the lyrics (with English translation) can be found in the "Postscript" of this book.

POSTSCRIPT

~

VOICES FROM AFRICA

"Though we cry, we still see through our tears."

(*African Proverb*)

AN AFRICAN WOMAN SPEAKS
FROM THE HEART

The manuscript for this book, *Six More Chances*, was completed on New Year's Day. Five days after the work was done, I requested the author to allow me to write a Preface to the book. For those who have known me, this was a very unusual request, since I've always preferred to stay out of the limelight. But I felt burdened to add my voice to the important message of the book.

I am pleased that the author gladly yielded to my plea. But he surprised me by offering me more than I had requested. Instead of a Preface to introduce the book, he elected to give me the last word in the Postscript! I'm truly honored to have been allowed to speak from my heart to the world.

In my world, I keep things simple and straightforward. And that's how I'll describe my personal reflections on the book. I do so from the perspective of one who, for decades, has been intimately acquainted with the author of *Six More Chances*.

MY SHARE OF SUCCESSES AND FAILURES

I have experienced joy, pain, sorrow, trials, and afflictions. Troubles, tribulations, challenges, scares, threats, and terrors have all come my way. Some have been physical; others have been mental, financial, and even spiritual. They have ranged in different degrees and lengths of time. They have evoked emotions from me that ranged from a numb or stoic acceptance to jubilation with reckless abandon.

In the language of this book, *Six More Chances*, I've had my own fair share of successes and failures and can therefore relate well to its contents.

Things happen in life that pit us against long-held beliefs, old friendships, future ambitions, and sometimes even ourselves. Often they are falls or failures that catch us completely off guard.

Sometimes we are the ones that tripped and fell. Other times it's others, including our loved ones. When the former happens, we know, or manufacture excusable reasons why our own failures *could* only have been so. Then our vision dims. When the latter happens, we know, or manufacture, justifiable reasons why the failures of others *should* not have been so. And our vision seems clear, when in reality it is just as obscure.

> WE NEED NOT FALL, BUT EVEN WHEN WE DO, HOPE IS NOT LOST.

Our hope lies in the all-encompassing love of a God That sees all failures, yours and mine, with greater than 20/20 acuity, yet loves us enough to clean us up and set us back on the track to success.

Failure is painfully real. Success is also incredibly real. *Six More Chances* packs a lot of details into one short book. It prepares the mind for the reality that temporary failures will continue to haunt us in this degenerate world. It balances this with the joyful reality of successes won, and yet to be won. Indeed, though painfully real, every failure can be transformed into success.

We can learn a lot from both failure and success, though experience teaches the wise that the former is sometimes the better teacher. A steadfast gaze on God bridges the huge divide between the two and unites them into unqualified success. We need not fall, but even when we do, hope is not lost.

It hurts to look at the scars from my own failures. It's equally painful to also trace the scars of loved ones from falls and failures, self-inflicted and otherwise. And the nail-scarred hands and feet of the One Who bore the full weight of our collective failures present a poignant reminder that I can't fix my failures by myself and can't fix yours for you, either. Likewise, you can't accomplish this for yourself or for me. He's chosen to fix them for me, and for you. His decision changes the whole landscape of failure, so I choose to look at all the falls and failures through the eyes of Him, the great FIXER.

PAINFUL RESPONSES TO THE FAILURES

In the words of our African elders, *"All lizards lie on their belly, but you don't know the ones with a bellyache."* This proverb aptly describes the discovery of foes among friends when the reality of failure hits home. It may sound petty to mention, but it's one of the important courses you learn in the school of failure!

And to assist in conveying that lesson to others who will face such things, I need to explain the dangers by way of testimony. For "though we cry, we still see through our tears."

Many people tried to goad me into responding to failure the way they wanted. But I chose to respond the way God wanted me to.

I was deeply pained by materials that were widely circulated by those who felt the author's admission of failure disqualified him from ever ministering again—certainly not in public ministry any time soon. I was dismayed by the intrigue that was employed. But I held my peace, referring the matter to the Lord.

I was also deeply wounded when I discovered that, without any direct efforts at clarification from the author, friends and former colleagues in ministry—some of whom we've known for at least two decades—did their best to publicize uncomplimentary material based largely on partial information and hearsay. I was equally saddened by how, on the basis of such materials, well-meaning individuals rendered judgment on the author's spiritual failure and response to it as evidence that he had committed the unpardonable sin against the Holy Spirit.

It was also horrifying to watch certain individuals and their organizations piously exploit the failures of others to advance their political agendas or to boost the survival of their organizations, caring little about the damage they caused to those already traumatized by failure.

My heart reached out in forgiveness to the offending ones who had fallen, and I prayed for them to experience true repentance. But I was taken aback by the conduct of some well-meaning counselors who tried to excuse the sin.

Some people wormed their way into my company—and into those of close friends and acquaintances—deliberately planting vile seeds intended to be harvested and juiced in order to poison any future ministry prospects of the author.

Through all of this, I responded the way I've watched my ancestral mothers respond; for when the African woman feels helpless and fallen, she lifts up her voice in supplication and cries out to God for help in what I choose to call the primordial prayer. I said a countless number of those. And He has been a great help to me. I said countless supplications and cries. I'll share one with you.

THE AFRICAN WOMAN'S PRIMORDIAL PRAYER

In the face of serious crisis and pain, she is usually without a voice, left to mourn her helplessness and loss with a seeming dignity that belies the anguish of her soul. Her pain comes from deep within her, the temporary storage of the grief of another bound to her heart by blood or water. At such times, the "how" does not make a difference; it is the "who" that counts.

Stunned with grief, comments are barred from escaping her lips and tears doomed to swim in the depths of her eyes without escape. It is a terrible time, so to get away from the crushing weight of her agony, if a Christian, she turns to Her Creator to pour out her misery. By this stage the objectives of her prayers are dualized to give meaning and comfort to her grief while she intercedes for that other person.

This is usually offered as bitter tears interspersed with deep groans pulsating with grief. Rarely is she able to form words, yet God answers, for He understands the language of tears as well as any other. She loses herself in her two-way conversation, praying for herself in one breath and stepping into the shoes of her wounded loved one in the other; desperate for comfort … seeking for healing … grasping at hope …

> WE KNEEL IN TEARS AND RISE UP WITH TEARS, A LITTLE COMFORTED, YET NEEDING MORE. THERE IS AT THE CORE OF THE AVERAGE AFRICAN WOMAN AN INNATE NEED FOR SUNSHINE AFTER RAIN AND LIGHT AT THE END OF TUNNELS.

The prayer here is a collection of Bible verses strung together in ways that we African women pray. Sometimes it seems as though we are distracted from our prayers. But no. The focus of our prayers remains upon the one for whom our heart grieves, and we speak to and for that other in anguished supplication to the Lord. We kneel in tears and rise up with tears, a little comforted, yet needing more.

Whether as grandmother, mother, sister, wife, daughter, or friend, there is at the core of the average African woman an innate need for sunshine after rain and light at the end of tunnels. The only bridge we've known to use to cross the chasm that often separates these realities is prayer, and somehow it ends up coming out. It's also the only bridge that's not been washed away … the only one that still works!

PSALM 34:17-19: *"The Lord hears His people when they call to Him for help. He rescues them from all their troubles. The Lord is close to the brokenhearted; He rescues those whose spirits are crushed. The righteous person faces many troubles, but the Lord comes to the rescue each time."*

PROV. 24:10: *"If you fail under pressure, your strength is too small."*

So, PSALM 20:1–3: *"In times of trouble, may the Lord answer your cry. May the name of the God of Jacob keep you safe from all harm. May He send you help from His sanctuary and strengthen you from Jerusalem. May He remember all your gifts and look favorably on your burnt offerings."*

PSALM 37:23, 24: *"The Lord directs the steps of the godly. He delights in every detail of their lives. Though they stumble, they will never fall, for the Lord holds them by the hand."*

Therefore, PROV. 24:15–18: *"Don't wait in ambush at the home of the godly, and don't raid the house where the godly live. The godly may trip seven times, but they will get up again. But one disaster is enough to overthrow the wicked. Don't rejoice when your enemies fall; don't be happy when they stumble. For the Lord will be displeased with you and will turn His anger away from them."*

PSALM 25: 15–21: *"My eyes are always on the Lord, for He rescues me from the traps of my enemies. Turn to me and have mercy, for I am alone and in deep distress. My problems go from bad to worse. Oh, save me from them all! Feel my pain and see my trouble. Forgive all my sins. See how many enemies I have and how viciously they hate me! Protect me! Rescue my life from them! Do not let me be disgraced, for in You I take refuge. May integrity and honesty protect me, for I put my hope in You."*

PSALM 35:10–12: *"With every bone in my body I will praise Him: 'Lord, who can compare with You? Who else rescues the helpless from the strong? Who else protects the helpless and poor from those who rob them?' Malicious witnesses testify against me. They accuse me of crimes I know nothing about. They repay me evil for good. I am sick with despair."*

PSALM 28:1–3: *"I pray to You, O Lord, my Rock. Do not turn a deaf ear to me. For if You are silent, I might as well give up and die. Listen to my prayer for mercy as I cry out to You for help, as I lift my hands toward Your holy sanctuary. Do not drag me away with the wicked—with those who do evil—those who speak friendly words to their neighbors while planning evil in their hearts."*

MICAH 7:7–10: *"As for me, I look to the Lord for help. I wait confidently for God to save me, and my God will certainly hear me. Do not gloat over me, my enemies! For though I fall, I will rise again. Though I sit in darkness, the Lord will be my Light. I will be patient as the Lord punishes me, for I have sinned against Him. But after that, He will take up my case and give me justice for all I have suffered from my enemies. The Lord will bring me into the light, and I will see His righteousness. Then my enemies will see that the Lord is on my side. They will be ashamed that they taunted me, saying, 'So where is the Lord—that God of yours?' With my own eyes I will see their downfall; they will be trampled like mud in the streets."*

PSALM 34:1–8: *"I will praise the Lord at all times. I will constantly speak His praises. I will boast only in the Lord; let all who are helpless take heart. Come, let us tell of the Lord's greatness; let us exalt His name together. I prayed to the Lord, and He answered me. He freed me from all my fears. Those who look to Him for help will be radiant with joy; no shadow of shame will darken their faces. In my desperation I prayed, and the Lord listened; He saved me from all my troubles. For the angel of the Lord is a guard; He surrounds and defends all who fear Him. Taste and see that the Lord is good. Oh, the joys of those who take refuge in Him!"*

> GOD IS BIGGER THAN YOUR FAILURES, AND HE
> CAN HELP YOU BACK ON THE ROAD TO SUCCESS,
> NO MATTER HOW DEEPLY YOU FALL.

I've sat through many book-writing sessions of the author of *Six More Chances* while offering silent prayers behind the scenes for inspiration and guidance. I can tell you in all honesty that none has been as intense as the one that led to what you now hold in your hands.

I've watched his many falls, false starts, and failures over the years; been privy to the refining process of the Master Potter as He's worked on this His clayey son. No other process could have produced that which he is today.

I've recounted my own failures, alongside his—failures of bad decisions, bad actions and attitudes, of sickness, of near-death, among others. The combined lessons from those painful experiences have produced instructional material I couldn't have learned otherwise. Thus, I have come to appreciate Success and Failure as two valuable teachers in life, with the latter being the better one—since its lessons are not easily forgotten.

The book you now hold in your hands, *Six More Chances*, reproduces briefly some of the lessons that have been learned in the fiery furnace of failure. They are meant to encourage, guide, uplift, instruct, and place hope ever before you that God is bigger than your failures, and He can help you back on the road to Success, no matter how deeply you fall.

It happened to me. It happened in my home. I chose to trust. I remained hopeful. You hold the evidence in your hands that God can help us succeed, in spite of having failed. I pray this will be your testimony, as well.

I am the author's wife of over three decades.

M'akoma Ahye Ma!

—*Rebecca Koranteng-Pipim,*
January 5, 2012

AN AFRICAN MUSICIAN SINGS FROM THE HEART

M'akoma Ahye Ma!

("My Heart Is Full!")

The phrase *"M'akoma Ahye Ma"* is from one of the Ghanaian languages, and literally means "My Heart Is Full!" It captures the mood of inexpressible joy, especially of an elevated or spiritual kind.

"M'akoma Ahye Ma" is also the title of an original musical composition that was dedicated to the author of *Six More Chances* by a leading Ghanaian composer when he heard of the author's experience of failure.

> THE PHRASE "M'AKOMA AHYE MA"
> IS FROM ONE OF THE GHANAIAN LANGUAGES,
> AND LITERALLY MEANS "MY HEART IS FULL!"
> IT CAPTURES THE MOOD OF INEXPRESSIBLE
> JOY, ESPECIALLY OF AN ELEVATED
> OR SPIRITUAL KIND.

The composer of this spiritually uplifting classical choral music is Newlove Annan, a Ghanaian currently pursuing a PhD in Ethnomusicology at the University of California at Los Angeles (UCLA). He comes from three generations of prominent Methodist ministers in Ghana and has composed over 900 pieces of sacred music. He is also the first Black African with compositions in a United Methodist hymnal, and the composer of the theme song for the 2004 U.S. World Council of Churches meeting held in Atlanta, Georgia.

In a letter to the author of Six More Chances, the composer of *"M'akoma Ahye Ma"* ("My Heart Is Full") explained that the song is his "thank-you" and encouragement to the author. "Thank-you" because at a very critical time in his own life, one of the author's sermons ("The Son of David") transformed his life. The song is offered to the author of this book as an encouragement during his painful ordeal of spiritual failure.

The basic thrust of *"M'akoma Ahye Ma"* ("My Heart Is Full") is summed up by the composer thus:

> *"I fell into the chaotic domain of the wicked enemy. Painful though it was, the experience has also revealed to me the power of God in Jesus Christ. It is this fact that makes my heart full of joy to the brim."*

The Music

The *"M'akoma Ahye Ma"* musical piece is woven out of precompositional elements (in nuggets) from Wolfgang Amadeus Mozart's "Lacrimosa," Johann Sebastian Bach's "Air on a G String," a Ghanaian "Worship Song," and the composer's own creativity for the most part. However, *"M'akoma Ahye Ma"* is an original work through and through.

Scriptural Background

The Scriptural references (NKJV) that form the backdrop to this classical choral composition are:

ACTS 2:25, 26
> *I foresaw the Lord always before my face,*
> *For He is at my right hand, that I may not be shaken.*
> *Therefore my heart rejoiced, and my tongue was glad;*
> *Moreover my flesh also will rest in hope.*

PSALM 103:1–5
> *Bless the Lord, O my soul;*
> *And all that is within me, bless His holy name!*
> *Bless the Lord, O my soul,*
> *And forget not all His benefits:*
> *Who forgives all your iniquities,*

Who heals all your diseases,
Who redeems your life from destruction,
Who crowns you with lovingkindness and tender mercies,
Who satisfies your mouth with good things,
So that your youth is renewed like the eagle's.

PSALM 8:4

"What is man that You are mindful of him,
And the son of man that You visit him?

PSALM 140

Deliver me, O Lord, from evil men;
Preserve me from violent men,
Who plan evil things in their hearts;
They continually gather together for war.
They sharpen their tongues like a serpent;
The poison of asps is under their lips. Selah.

Keep me, O Lord, from the hands of the wicked;
Preserve me from violent men,
Who have purposed to make my steps stumble.
The proud have hidden a snare for me, and cords;
They have spread a net by the wayside;
They have set traps for me. Selah.

I said to the Lord: "You are my God;
Hear the voice of my supplications, O Lord.
O God the Lord, the Strength of my salvation,
You have covered my head in the day of battle.
Do not grant, O Lord, the desires of the wicked;
Do not further his wicked scheme,
Lest they be exalted. Selah.

"As for the head of those who surround me,
Let the evil of their lips cover them;
Let burning coals fall upon them;

Let them be cast into the fire,
Into deep pits, that they rise not up again.
Let not a slanderer be established in the earth;
Let evil hunt the violent man to overthrow him."
I know that the Lord will maintain
The cause of the afflicted,
And justice for the poor.
Surely the righteous shall give thanks to Your name;
The upright shall dwell in Your presence.

2 TIMOTHY 4:8

Finally, there is laid up for me the crown of righteousness, which the Lord,
the righteous Judge, will give to me on that Day, and not to me only but also
to all who have loved His appearing.

The Words (Lyrics)

The text of the music is in the Twi language of Ghana. Translation into English is by the composer.

NOTE: An "e" with an apostrophe after it (e') is pronounced like the "e" in the word "egg." Similarly, an "o" with an apostrophe after it (o') is pronounced like the "o" in the word "or." The proper noun "Nyame" is a reference to Deity and can be translated as "God" or "the Lord." An "hy" combination is pronounced like "sh" in the word "shoe." And a "ky" combination is pronounced like the "ch" in "cheese."

To listen to or download the *"M'akoma Ahye Ma!"* music, go to:
www.TheWoundedEagleBooks.com

M'AKOMA AHYE MA
(My Heart Is Full)
Music, Words & Translation © by Newlove Annan

TWI

Oh! M'akoma ahye' ma Nyame mu;
Me kra di dew wo' Nyame mu,
Me sunsum di ahurusi Nyame mu,
Oh, me kra to dwom de'de'
yi Wo Nyame aye' daa.

Repeat

Oh, me mu ade nyinaa,
yi wo Nyame aye';
Fa w'aye'ye'de ye' dwom to,
na yi N'aye' daa daa.
O-nipa ne hwan koraa,
na Nyame aniku ne ho?
O'hwe' me so, kyre' me kwan, hyira me,
Oh, me kra yi wo Nyame aye',
Fa w'aseda bra Nyame anim,
na to ayeyi dwom ma ne din daa.

Repeat

Oh, me kra, yi N'a ye',
Oh, m'akoma di a' hrusi,
na da wo Nyame ase,
Fa w'aseda ye' naase,
Ma w'akoma nye' ma mbu so!

M'akoma ahye' ma, m'akoma ahye' ma,
M'akoma ahye' ma, m'akoma ahye' ma,
ahye' ma.
M'akoma ahye' ma, M'akoma ahye' ma,
M'akoma ahye' ma, M'akoma ahye' ma,
ahye' ma.

ENGLISH

Oh! My heart is full in the Lord;
My soul rejoices in the Lord,
My spirit is glad in the Lord,
Oh, my soul, sing beautiful songs,
in praise of your Lord always.

Repeat

Oh, all that is within me,
praise your Lord;
Offer your songs of gratitude,
and praise Him always.
Who really is man,
that the Lord is so mindful of him?
He cares for me, shows me the way, blesses me,
Oh, my soul, praise your Lord,
Present your thanks before the Lord,
and sing songs of praises to His name always.

Repeat

Oh, my soul, praise Him,
Oh, my heart, be glad,
and give thanks to your Lord,
Transform your "thank-yous" into thanksgiving,
Let your heart be full beyond its brim!

My heart is full, my heart is full,
My heart is full, my heart is full,
it's full.
My heart is full, my heart is full,
My heart is full, my heart is full,
it's full.

M'ako'to' Bonsam asro'kye no mu,
Afei mahu Jesus, s'Otumi gye nkwa,
M'akoma ahye' ma.

I have fallen into the tempest of Satan,
Now I've found Jesus, that He is able to save,
My heart is full.

M'ako'to' Bonsam asro'kye no mu,
Afei mahu Jesus s'Otumi gye nkwa,
M'akoma ahye' ma, ahye' ma abuso.
M'akoma ahye' ma, m'akoma ahye' ma abuso.
M'ako'to' Bonsam asro'kye no mu,
Afei mahu Jesus s'Otumi gye nkwa,
M'akoma ahye' ma, ahye' ma abuso.

I have fallen into the tempest of Satan,
Now I've found Jesus, that He's able to save,
My heart is full, it's full to overflowing.
My heart is full, my heart is full to overflowing.
I have fallen into the tempests of Satan,
Now I've found Jesus, that He's able to save,
My heart is full, it's full to overflowing.

M'ako'to' Bonsam asro'kye no mu,
Afei mahu Jesus s'Otumi gye nkwa,
M'akoma ahye' ma, ahye' ma abuso.
M'akoma ahye' ma, m'akoma ahye' ma abuso.
M'ako'to' Bonsam asro'kye no mu,
Afei mahu Jesus s'Otumi gye nkwa,
M'akoma ahye' ma, ahye' ma abuso.

I have fallen into the tempest of Satan,
Now I've found Jesus, that He's able to save,
My heart is full, it's full to overflowing.
My heart is full, my heart is full to overflowing.
I have fallen into the tempests of Satan,
Now I've found Jesus, that He's able to save,
My heart is full, it's full to overflowing.

Instrumentals

Instrumentals

Oh, me kra, so're yi N'aye',
Fa w'ayeyi dwom bre' No.
Fa w'akoma mu dwom bre' No,
O'no na wagye Wo nkwa.
O'no na wagye Wo nkwa.
O'no na o'sa wo ya re;
O'no na wapagya wo,
O'no na o'de wo si yie, daa daa,
O'no na o'hwe' wo so,
W'agyew' afi nkoa som',
na o'de wo nan si botan so.

Oh, my soul, rise up and praise Him,
Bring your thanksgiving songs to Him.
Bring your heartfelt songs to Him,
He's the One Who has saved your life.
He's the One Who has saved your life.
He's the One Who has healed your diseases;
He's the One Who has lifted you up,
He's the One Who establishes you, always,
He's the One Who cares for you,
Redeemed you from bondage,
and has planted your feet on solid rock.

Oh, me kra, yi N'a ye',
Oh, me kra da N'a se,
Oh, me kra, tontom No,
Pagya No, ma No so!
E'ye' O'no n'o'de Ne kra to ho' ma wo,
So're, som no.

Oh, my soul, praise Him,
Oh, my soul, thank Him,
Oh, my soul, laud Him,
Lift Him up, exalt Him!
He's the One Who laid down His life for you,
Rise up, worship Him.

M'ako'to' Bonsam asro'kye no mu,
Afei mahu Jesus s'Otumi gye nkwa,
M'akoma ahye' ma, ahye' ma abuso.
M'akoma ahye' ma, ahye' ma abuso.
M'ako'to' Bonsam asro'kye no mu,
Afei mahu Jesus s'Otumi gye nkwa,
M'akoma ahye' ma, ahye' ma abuso.

I have fallen into the tempests of Satan,
Now I've found Jesus, that He's able to save,
My heart is full, it's full to overflowing.
My heart is full, it's full to overflowing.
I have fallen into the tempests of Satan,
Now I've found Jesus, that He's able to save,
My heart is full, it's full to overflowing.

To listen to or download the *"M'akoma Ahye Ma!"* music, go to:
www.TheWoundedEagleBooks.com

"A RIGHTEOUS MAN
MAY FALL SEVEN TIMES
AND RISE AGAIN..."
— Proverbs 24:16, NKJV

RESOURCES BY THE AUTHOR

~

If *Six More Chances* has been a blessing to you, you will also greatly appreciate some of the other insightful books by the author. (Information about how to obtain them is found at the end of this section.)

AUTHOR'S BOOK ON TRIALS AND AFFLICTIONS

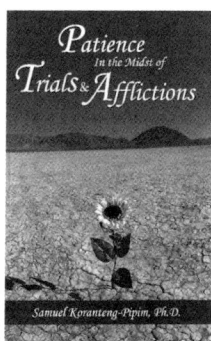

Patience in the Midst of Trials

In the journey through life, trials await us all. For at one point or another, every one of us is bound to experience the agony of pain, disappointment, sorrow, hurt, loss, or some other form of suffering that will severely test our resiliency and character. We may also suffer afflictions—prolonged ordeals of suffering that lie deeper in the soul. God uses these trials and afflictions to cultivate in us the virtue of patience.

You can tell that the Lord is developing patience in you when you run into many anguishing experiences; when the things or people you depend on suddenly fail you; when your life seems to be in detours; when prolonged illness and other forms of affliction plague you; when your situation in life goes from bad to worse. Above all, you know you are being schooled in patience when you cry out to God for help, and He doesn't seem to hear or care.

Patience in the Midst of Trials and Afflictions insightfully explains the nature of patience, why God permits trials and afflictions, and how you can benefit from them. This life-changing book will be a source of encouragement to you and your loved ones. It will give you confidence in God's guidance and renew your determination to trust Him, no matter what.

ISBN: 1-890014-04-4. Price: $10.99

AUTHOR'S BOOK ON LOVE

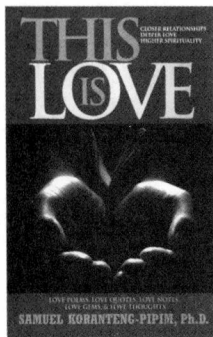

This Is Love

Love. It's the never-ending, driving quest—the all-consuming need—the motivating desire—of every man, woman, and child on Earth.

But just what *is* love? Is it accurately defined by the sum total of all the song lyrics, love poems, and love stories ever written? All the movies ever filmed? All the dramas ever acted?

Toward a deeper, more satisfying answer to the question "What is love?" the *This Is Love* book manuscript contains a distilled, carefully chosen sampling of poems, quotations, articles and essays, stories, and personal reflections focused on love.

Some of the material in these pages is original with the author. Some represents the best thoughts of other writers. Found here are the words of those divinely inspired and those who have simply shared their own ideas. But in a search for the true definition of love, where *This Is Love* best succeeds is in its undeviating focus on the Source of all real love—the One Whose name is synonymous with love.

Real love cannot exist outside of a relationship. And whether ours is horizontal, involving other people around us—or vertical, between us and our God—or both, this book will open new vistas of understanding and delight as readers take in its pages.

ISBN: 978-1890014-08-7; Price: $12.99

AUTHOR'S BOOK ON INTEGRITY

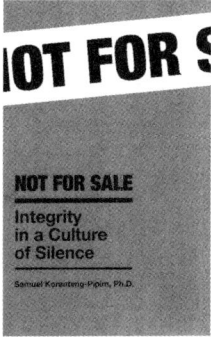

Not for Sale

Not for Sale is a call to daily self-examination—and action. It highlights the consequences of the cowardly silence all too often displayed by some otherwise good and well-meaning people.

Contending that silence, neutrality, or indifference in times of crisis is a criminal act, if not a betrayal of faith, this book makes an urgent plea against choosing to do nothing in the face of wrong-doing. It's a thoughtful yet impassioned appeal to redis-cover the strength and power of integrity and principle.

This volume challenges men and women—especially those with the energy and idealism of youth—to claim the moral high ground in their lives. The character crisis cries out for those who cannot be silenced by fear, threat, or intimidation. It cries out for those who cannot be lured to cowardice or compromise by blandishments of money, prestige, or power. It cries out for those who will stand boldly—and state emphatically—that they are *Not for Sale*.

ISBN: 978-1890014-09-4; Price: $17.99

AUTHOR'S BOOK ON STEWARDSHIP AND FAITH

God Is Faithful

You can give without loving but you cannot love without giving. This is why the Bible gives considerable attention to financial stewardship. Every one of us, whether rich or poor, has been invited to give generously in response to the Lord s grace. Honoring such an invitation is, however, not always easy.

In this small volume, *God Is Faithful,* you will discover why financial stewardship is a journey of faith and a test of commitment. The book also reveals how God has promised to take care of all your needs if you trust Him with your material possessions.

ISBN: 978-1890014-07-0; Price: $5.00

AUTHOR'S BOOK ON CHOICES & THEIR CONSEQUENCES

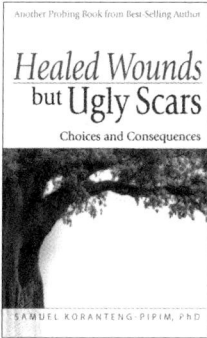

Healed Wounds but Ugly Scars

Wrong choices. Bad decisions. Painful Wounds. Whether self-inflicted or caused by others, pain is a part of life we all experience. And while there is always forgiveness for our sins, the consequences are not always removed. Our wounds may heal, but the ugly scars remain.

Healed Wounds but Ugly Scars is intended to caution against making wrong choices in our journey through life choices that have far-reaching consequences for ourselves and others. More importantly, the book is designed to help us retrace our steps back to healing, to lead us to the One Who alone can help us live with our ugly scars.

ISBN: 978-1890014-11-7; Price: $14.99

For these and other resources contact:

Remnant Publications
649 East Chicago Road
Coldwater, MI 49036
Tel. 1-800-423-1319
www.remnantpublications.com

For quantity discounts to churches, schools, or groups, contact the author through the above information, or through:

info@EAGLESonline.org;
www.TheWoundedEagleBooks.com

ENDNOTES

Introduction

1. Tim Eyre, "The Upside of Failure: The Dividends of Understanding and Embracing You Failures." http://www.pickthebrain.com/blog/the-upside-of-failure/ (accessed December 29, 2011).

2 http://drpipim.org/thought-nuggets.html.

Chapter 1: Success in the Midst of Failure

1 Giselle Mahoro's Graduation Message, December 18, 2011, The University of Michigan, Ann Arbor, Michigan.

2 CAMPUS stands for Center for Adventist Ministry to Public University Students. A division of the Michigan Conference Public Campus Ministries Department, CAMPUS is based in Ann Arbor, Michigan, near The University of Michigan. CAMPUS describes its approach to ministry in the following way: (1) *Vision*: A Bible-based revival movement, in which every student is a missionary; (2) *Methodology*: Biblical simplicity; (3) Philosophy: Academic excellence and spiritual excellence; (4) *Goal*: Double our membership every year; (5) *Watchword*: Each one reach one; (6) *Mission*: To prepare secular university campuses for the imminent return of Christ; (7) *Motto*: Taking Higher Education Higher. For more information, see www.campushope.com.

3 CAMPUS runs a Missionary Training Program in Ann Arbor, Michigan, near The University of Michigan campus. It is a two-semester, hands-on program that combines sound classroom instruction with practical field training in ministry and outreach activities. Dedicated staff and guest instructors teach the classes. The goal of the Missionary Training Program is to develop godly and effective leaders, brilliant and winsome soulwinners, and sound spiritual counselors for college/university campuses and other professional environments. Limited to no more than a dozen serious students at a time, the program duration overlaps with the academic year at The University of Michigan.

4 "Our duty to act as missionaries for God in the very position where He has placed us has been greatly overlooked by us as a people" *Testimonies for the Church* 5:184.4.

5 "Did the professed believers in the truth live the truth, they would today all be missionaries. Some would be working in the islands of the sea; some, in the different countries of the world. Some would be serving Christ as home missionaries. Not all are called upon to go abroad. Some may be successful in business lines, and in this work they may represent Christ. They may show to the world that business may be conducted on righteous principles, in strict fidelity to the truth. There may be Christian lawyers, Christian physicians, Christian merchants. Christ may be represented in all lawful callings."—Manuscript 19, 1900 (*Welfare Ministry*, p. 111.4).

6 *Testimonies for the Church* 4:12.1.

7 Among his well-known inventions were bifocals, the Franklin stove, the glass "armonica," the lightning rod, and the odometer. With respect to the bifocals, it was known that Benjamin Franklin had poor vision and needed glasses to read. He got tired of constantly taking them off and putting them back on, so he decided to figure out a way to make his glasses let him see both near and far. He had two pairs of spectacles cut in half and put half of each lens in a single frame. Today, we call them bifocals.

8 Charles Swindoll, *Hand Me Another Brick*, Thomas Nelson, 1978, pp. 82, 83, and *Bits & Pieces*, November, 1989, p. 12. See also, "Tragedy," Sermon Illustrations, http://www.sermonillustrations.com/a-z/d/disaster.htm.

9 We know, of course, that Steve Jobs didn't go up into literal clouds or to Heaven at his death. The quip was a witty or humorous remark linking his death with the iCloud invention. The Bible says all who die are resting in their graves, awaiting the Second Coming of Christ, when there will be a resurrection—to eternal life or eternal damnation. (See, for example, John 5:25, 28, 29; Acts 2:29, 34.) See a discussion of "Beyond Ultimate Failure" in chapter 3 of this book.

10 http://news.stanford.edu/news/2005/june15/jobs-061505.html.

11 After Jobs' death the original Apple "Think Different" commercial resurfaced. In it, images of transformative people throughout the 20th century are shown as a narrator toasts them for changing the world. In the versions that aired on TV, the narrator is Richard Dreyfuss. But in the version quoted above the narrator is Steve Jobs himself. He narrated that statement in 1997. See http://appadvice.com/appnn/2011/10/petition-asks-apple-to-air-steve-jobs-narrated-crazy-ones-ad.

12 Eurice Ed C. Mangaoang, "Failure": A Stepping Stone to Success (http://ryuzakieur.blogspot.com/2010/10/failure-stepping-stone-to-success.html [accessed December 25, 2011]).

13 Micah 7:8–10, 18, 19; Psalm 37:23, 24; Luke 2:34; Revelation 1:18.

14 Romans 5:3, 4; Hebrews 12:7–11; 2 Corinthians 4:8, 9.

15 Isaiah 43:18.

16 For most people success is defined in terms of achieving goals, acquiring wealth, and having prestige, favor, status, and power. The "successful" people are those who enjoy the "good life"—understood to mean being financially secure, emotionally secure, being surrounded by admirers, and enjoying the fruits of their labor. Success only seems to deal with the "here and now." Anyone who does not fulfill these measures of success is considered a failure. But in the Word of God, success is faithfulness (Joshua 1:8; Proverbs 21:21; 2 Corinthians 3:4–6).

17 Over the years there have been many different variations of the "One Solitary Life" poem. The version reproduced here is my own, adapted and conflated from many different versions currently in circulation. For a summary discussion of the authorship and versions of this poem, see my *This Is Love*, (Ann Arbor, Michigan: Berean Books, 2007) pp. 92–94, notes 1 and 2.

18 *The Ministry of Healing*, p. 487.3.

Chapter 2: True Success & Apparent Failure

1 The preamble of our official Fundamental Beliefs begins with the words, "Seventh-day Adventists accept the Bible as their only creed and hold certain fundamental beliefs to be the teaching of the Holy Scriptures." We embrace some 28 fundamental beliefs to constitute the church's understanding and expression of the teaching of Scripture. Of these, the Bible's sole authority is listed as #1. It reads: "The Holy Scriptures, Old and New Testaments, are the written Word of God, given by divine inspiration through holy men of God who spoke and wrote as they were moved by the Holy Spirit. In this Word, God has committed to man the knowledge necessary for salvation. The Holy Scriptures are the infallible revelation of His will. They are the standard of character, the test of experience, the authoritative revealer of doctrines, and the trustworthy record of God's acts in history. (2 Peter 1:20, 21; 2 Tim. 3:16, 17; Ps. 119:105; Prov. 30:5, 6; Isa. 8:20; John 17:17; 1 Thess. 2:13; Heb. 4:12.)." See http://www.adventist.org/beliefs/fundamental/index.html.

2 Although in this book I have tried to give proper credit for these sources, if perchance I have used a quotation, sentence, thought, or expression of others without giving due credit, I offer my heartfelt apologies ... and thanks!

3 Charles Spurgeon, *Commenting and Commentaries* (New York: Sheldon, 1876), p. 62.

4 E. G. White (1827–1915) was a woman of remarkable spiritual gifts who lived most of her life during the 19th century, yet through her writings and public ministry she has made a revolutionary impact on millions of people around the world. She was a contemporary of Christian giants like Dwight L. Moody (1837–1899), F. B. Meyer

(1847–1929), Henry Drummond (1851–1897), R. A. Torrey (1856–1928), Ralph Connor (1860–1937), Charles Spurgeon (1834–1892), and Oswald Chambers (1874–1917). During Ellen G. White's lifetime, she wrote more than 5,000 periodical articles and 49 books. Today, including compilations from her manuscripts, more than 100 titles are available in English. She is the most translated woman writer in the entire history of literature and the most translated American author of either gender, measured by the number of languages having at least one of her works. Her literary productions deal with a wide range of subjects: spirituality, theology, education, health, family, etc. But she was more than a prolific author. While the world is only now coming to appreciate her deep spiritual and practical insights, millions have always recognized her as a recipient of the true gift of prophecy. Her life-changing masterpiece on successful Christian living, *Steps to Christ*, has been published in about 150 languages, with well over tens of millions of copies in circulation. The book deals with the central issue of how to become and remain a Christian: the concern at the core of Mrs. White's voluminous writing. Mrs. White's crowning literary achievement is the five-volume "Conflict of the Ages" series, which traces the conflict between good and evil from its origin to its dramatic, soon-to-unfold conclusion. It is widely acclaimed as the best devotional commentary on the entire Bible. Ellen G. White came from a Methodist background and became one of the pioneers of the Seventh-day Adventist Church, one of the fastest growing Protestant denominations in the world. In this book, references to E. G. White's works are from the standard English editions of her published writings. See, https://egwwritings.org/.

5   *Gospel Workers*, p. 292.1.

6   Ibid., p. 292.2.

7   *Selected Messages*, bk. 2, p. 167.1.

8   *Christ's Object Lessons*, p. 353.1

9   *Patriarchs and Prophets*, p. 602.1.

10 *Manuscript Releases* 9:388.0.

11 *Manuscript Releases* 21:400.1.

12 *Testimonies for the Church* 5:754.1.

13 *Messages to Young People*, p. 150.1.

14 *Prophets and Kings*, p. 486.3.

15 *Testimonies for the Church* 5:158.

16 *Prophets and Kings*, p. 486.2.

17 *Christ's Object Lessons*, p. 363.1.

18 *The Adventist Home*, p. 367.1.

19 *The Review and Herald*, July 30, 1901, par. 14.

20 *Colporteur Ministry*, p. 107.5.

21 *The Adventist Home*, p. 391.1.

22 *Counsels to Parents and Teachers*, p. 422.4.

23 *Education*, p. 262.1.

24 *A Call to Stand Apart* (a paraphrase), p. 99.8.

25 *Sons and Daughters of God,* p. 254.4.

26 *Counsels to Parents and Teachers,* p. 21.1.

27 *The Review and Herald, September* 25, 1883, par. 13.

28 Pamphlet 149, p. 20.2.

29 *The Review and Herald,* July 23, 1901, par. 8.

30 *The Ministry of Healing*, p. 143.3.

31 Ibid., pp. 366.3–367.1.

32 *Education*, p. 207.1.

33 *The Review and Herald,* April 6, 1886, par. 3.

34 Pamphlet 043, p. 26.0.

35 *Education*, p. 270.2.

36 *Gospel Workers,* p. 142.2.

37 Ibid., p. 269.2.

38 *The Upward Look*, p. 116.4.

39 *Life Sketches*, p. 245.1.

40 *The Ministry of Healing,* p. 200.3.

41 *Prophets and Kings,* p. 595.1, 2.

42 *The Desire of Ages*, pp. 678.3–680.0.

43 *The Ministry of Healing,* p. 487.3.

44 *Christ's Object Lessons,* p. 363.1 and *Messages to Young People,* p. 309.3.

45 *The Desire of Ages,* p. 490.5.

46 *Prophets and Kings,* p. 595.1, 2.

47 *Life Sketches,* p. 245.1.

48 *Gospel Workers*, p. 142.2.

50 *This Day With God*, p. 367.2.

51 *Testimonies to Ministers*, p. 323.1.

52 *Testimonies for the Church*, 5:158.

53 *Patriarchs and Prophets*, p. 657.2.

54 The Christian walk or Christian life is a *process* of spiritual growth. The person who is born again as a child of God does not remain a baby. As he is nourished by the Word of God, the child grows day by day until he matures into the full stature of our Lord Jesus Christ. The Christian experience is never flat or at a plateau. Either you are growing up or growing down. If you are not growing, you are regressing. Other expressions and imageries used in the New Testament for this Christian walk are: "following after righteousness" (1 Timothy 6:11), being "transformed" (Romans 12:2), "perfecting holiness" (2 Corinthians 7:1), "growing up ... into the full stature of Christ" (Ephesians 4:15), "pressing toward the mark" (Philippians 3:14), being "built up in Christ" (Colossians 2:7), becoming "complete in all the will of God" (Colossians 4:12), fighting "the good fight of faith" (1 Timothy 6:12; cf. v. 11), "partaking of the divine nature" (2 Peter 1:4), and "growing in grace" (2 Peter 3:18). In short, the Christian walk refers to living a holy or sanctified life. This walk of holiness is the only kind of life that fits a person for Heaven. Thus, we find in the Old Testament that "Enoch walked with God: and he was not; for God took him" (Gen. 5:24).

55 Several expressions are used in Scripture to describe the Christian walk: walking "in newness of life" (Romans 6:4), "walking by faith" (2 Corinthians 5:7), "walking in Him [Christ]" (Colossians 2:6), "walking in the Spirit" (Galatians 5:16), "walking in the light" (1 John 1:7), "walking in truth" (2 John 4), and "walking as children of light" (Ephesians 5:8).

56 "The apostle Peter had had a long experience in the things of God. His faith in God's power to save had strengthened with the years, *until he had proved beyond question that there is no possibility of failure before the one who*, advancing by faith, ascends round by round, ever upward and onward, to the topmost round of the ladder that reaches even to the portals of Heaven" (*The Acts of the Apostles*, p. 533.1).

57 *Manuscript Releases*, vol. 3, p. 68.1.

58 *The Spirit of Prophecy*, vol. 2, p. 244.1.

59 *The Review and Herald*, April 6, 1886, par. 2–4.

60 *True Education* (an adaptation of *Education*), p. 163.1.

61 Ibid., p. 163.2.

62 *The Ministry of Healing*, p. 482.1.

63 Ibid., p. 482.2.

64 Ibid., p. 143.3.

65 For a summary discussion of the arguments for both sides of the issue, see the April 6, 2011 blog of Stephen J. Gill, "Learn From Success or Learn From Failure: You Decide." http://stephenjgill.typepad.com/performance_improvement_b/2011/04/learn-from-success-or-learn-from-failure-you-decide.html (accessed December 25, 2011). Gill, who lives in Ann Arbor, Michigan, was on the faculty of The University of Michigan School of Education before becoming a full-time consultant on human performance improvement.

66 At the time of his article, Matias was serving as Research Assistant, at MIT Media Lab Center for Civic Media. See J. Nathan Matias, "Why Learn From Failure When You Can Learn From Success?" November 29, 2011; http://civic.mit.edu/blog/natematias/why-learn-from-failure-when-you-can-learn-from-success. (accessed December 25, 2011).

67 J. Nathan Matias, "Why Learn From Failure When You Can Learn From Success?" November 29, 2011; http://civic.mit.edu/blog/natematias/why-learn-from-failure-when-you-can-learn-from-success (accessed December 25, 2011). He writes: "This debate is especially important when we give advice to young people. Those who value failure encourage young people to start their own company or charity. Those who value success encourage apprenticeship first and serial entrepreneurship later. The argument for failure is based on an overly high respect for knowledge. In this view, perhaps new entrepreneurs will encounter records of informative failures and avoid the mistakes of the past. This view doesn't account for how people really learn, especially when they're gripped by the fire of a great idea they want to share with the world. In a mentoring relationship, few things are more tiresome than a mentor who simply dumps advice on the mentee. Learning, even when you have a personal mentor, is a much more complex dance. The nuances of recruiting, developing a customer base, or carrying out a design process are not easily turned into an 8-minute talk. They rely on capabilities rather than mere knowledge. Even were [sic] reports and talks are an effective way to learn, honest failure reports are hard to write. They're even harder to share outside one's own organisation. It's much easier to blame the marketing, models, or strategies than to blame a first mate who was a touch heavy on the grog. At other times, we blame others to preserve our ego, ignoring more basic flaws in our approach or organisation."

68 Ellen G. White, *Steps to Christ*, pp. 11.2–12.0.

69 White, *Steps to Christ*, p. 12.1. Note that I have reformatted the original paragraph so that the pronoun "He" stands out.

70 Again, I have reformatted the passage so that the pronoun referring to Christ stands out.

Chapter 3: Beyond Ultimate Failure

1 I am indebted to J. I. Packer and Carolyn Nystrom for some of the insights on hope. See their *Never Beyond Hope: How God Touches & Uses Imperfect People* (Downers Grove, Ill.: InterVarsity Press, 2000).

2 *Testimonies for the Church* 9:286.2–288.0.

Chapter 4: The Key to Success

1 God's moral Law (the Ten Commandments given in Exodus 20:1–17) summarizes how a person can show love to God and love to other human beings. These Ten Commandments are not "Ten Suggestions," for they are the foundation of God's government and the basis of society's wellbeing and happiness. I am not suggesting that we should keep the Law *in order to be saved.* For the Bible is very clear that anyone who is ever going to be saved will be saved by grace alone, through faith in Christ Jesus (Eph. 2:8ff.), But the Bible is also equally plain in its teaching that those who are saved by grace also keep the Law as *evidence* that they *have been saved: "And hereby we do know that we know Him, if we keep His commandments. He that saith, I know Him, and keepeth not His commandments, is a liar, and the truth is not in him"* (1 John 2:3, 4). *"By this we know that we love the children of God, when we love God, and keep His commandments. For this is the love of God, that we keep His commandments: and His commandments are not grievous"* (1 John 5:2, 3). This is why God's end-time church is described as that which keeps all of God's Ten Commandments: "Here is the patients of the saints. *Here are they who keep the commandments of God* and have the faith of Jesus" (Rev. 14:12). Scripture teaches that those who love the Lord will also keep all of His Ten Commandment Law, including the seventh-day Sabbath, which is Saturday (John 14:15). To disregard any one of the Ten Commandments is to disregard all (James 2:10, 11; cf. Matt. 5:17–19). Since the Decalogue is the transcript of God's character as reflected in the perfect life of our Lord Jesus Christ, we shall all be judged by this moral Law (James 2:12). Those who are going to be saved and, hence, have access to the tree of life will all lovingly keep God's Law (Rev. 22:14; cf. Matt. 19:17–19). Because "sin is the transgression of the law" (1 John 3:4), the breaking or transgression of any of God's moral Ten Commandment laws is an "immoral" act or a "moral failure."

2 The version reproduced here was originally published in a special 2007 GYC issue of Adventists Affirm. See David Asscherick, "Keep Getting Up: The Single Secret to Succeeding in the Christian Walk," Adventists Affirm, vol. 21, no. 3 (Fall 2007). I've only made some minor modifications in headings and paragraphing, sometimes dividing long paragraphs into shorter ones, without deleting anything from the published version. For the online version of the same message, see http://www.adventistsaffirm.org/article. php?id=211&search=asscherick (accessed December 29, 2011).

3   The original version read: "Judas betrayed Jesus for a pittance and soon thereafter fell, dan-
     gling horribly at the end of a noosed rope. Peter fell, too; he denied his Lord thrice, then
     lived for many more years during which he fell again and again (see, for example, Galatians
     2, where Peter reverts back to his bigoted ways in his relations with the Gentiles)."

4   Jesus isn't telling us to forgive our brothers 490 times or 70 x 7 instances, He's telling us
     we should always forgive our brothers when they have sinned against us. As many times
     as forgiveness is needed. An unlimited number of times. In Luke 17:3, 4, Jesus says,
     "So watch yourselves. If your brother or sister sins against you, rebuke them; and if they
     repent, forgive them. Even if they sin against you seven times in a day and seven times
     come back to you saying 'I repent,' you must forgive them" (NIV). God in Heaven has
     forgiven us all of humanity's sins. How wrong it would be for us to deny our brothers
     and sisters similar forgiveness for much lesser matters. The parable in Matthew 18:23–35
     reinforces this truth of the availability of God's unlimited forgiveness, a gift we are to
     pass on to others (Ephesians 6:32).

5   E. G. White, *Messages to Young People,* p. 99.4.

6   White, *Steps to Christ,* p. 64.1.

FURTHER READING

Six More Chances is about how we can transform failure into success. Those who seek to dig a little deeper into the subject will find the following two books very valuable:

HOW DO WE MOVE FROM SPIRITUAL FAILURE TO SUCCESS?

Steps to Christ for a Sanctified Life by E. G. White

How do we move from spiritual failure to success? *Steps to Christ for a Sanctified Life* deals with the central issue of how to become and remain a Christian. In just a few short chapters, the book will help you discover the steps in finding a forever Friend in Jesus. You'll read about His love for you, repentance, faith and acceptance, growing like Him, the privilege of prayer, what to do with doubt, and how to spend your days rejoicing with your newfound Friend, Jesus.

What about dealing with failure? Many people who give their hearts to the Lord are as little babes just beginning to walk—so excited at that first step. But unlike the baby who falls and gets up to try and try again until he or she walks without falling, many Christians are frustrated and discouraged at the failings of their walk with God and do not continue to move forward.

Now you will be able to put together the pieces of your puzzled life and have peace in your heart. When you search for the path that leads to Jesus and find Him, you won't have to get discouraged. *Steps to Christ for a Sanctified Life* will lead you in a direction to discover the secrets to successful Christian living and to experience true Christian maturity.

This work by E. G. White is a masterpiece on successful Christian living. It contains her book *Steps to Christ*, which has been published in about 150 languages, with well over tens of millions of copies in circulation.

Price: $9.95

BEYOND ULTIMATE FAILURE:
DEATH, AFTERLIFE, AND SPIRITUALISM

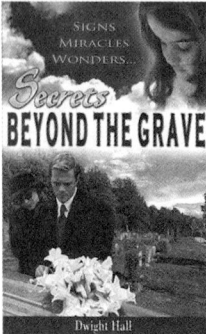

Secrets Beyond the Grave by Dwight Hall

Today, the confusion surrounding the afterlife is more widespread than ever, causing heartache for millions who have lost loved ones. Moreover, Hollywood and television are now focusing intensely on the spirit world, but are their fantastical portrayals just imagination ... or are they grounded in reality?

The bottom line is that everyone wants to know what happened to their loved ones. Are they happy? Are they safe? How can we be sure they're not in Hell? Can they visit us from beyond the grave, and how do we know that ghostly spirits have purely benevolent motives?

Secrets Beyond the Grave has the straightforward answers to these and other questions that you want and need to know. Dwight teams up with one of America's most published and translated authors, E. G. White, to steer you through the fog of confusion and reveal the stunning secrets that lie just beyond the grave.

Grounded on the truth taught by Jesus you'll find true peace regarding your loved ones, giving you confidence for the future and enabling you to overcome the darkest fears we all must face.

ISBN: 9-781-883012-36-6; Price: $9.95

For these and other resources contact:

Remnant Publications
649 East Chicago Road
Coldwater, MI 49036
Tel. 1-800-423-1319
www.remnantpublications.com

For quantity discounts to churches, schools, or groups, contact the author through the above information, or through:

info@EAGLESonline.org;
www.TheWoundedEagleBooks.com

ABOUT THE AUTHOR

Samuel Koranteng Pipim, PhD—a U.S.-based Ghanaian author, inspirational speaker, and advocate for youth empowerment—was trained in engineering and systematic theology. He is currently the Director of a Center for Leadership Development known as EAGLES (Empowerment and Advisory Group for Leadership, Excellence, and Service). Dr. Pipim has authored and co-authored about sixteen books—including his bestselling works *Patience in the Midst of Trials and Afflictions*, *Healed Wounds but Ugly Scars*, and *Not for Sale*. He has spoken extensively around the world at events for youth, students, and young professionals. His public Bible lectures on a wide variety of subjects are presented in a winsome, dynamic, and crystal clear way that engages both the hearts and minds of his audiences, whether secular or religious. For 12 years, he served as a Director of Public Campus Ministries, ministering to students, faculty, and staff at The University of Michigan. In that role, he grandfathered and mentored influential grassroots youth and young adult organizations around the world. Besides currently directing the EAGLES Center (www.EAGLESonline.org), Dr. Pipim also serves as a special consultant on Bible projects for Remnant Publications.